D1209401

LISBON

JOURNEYS AND STORIES

PEDRO VELOSO / SUSANA FONSECA / SÉRGIO FONSECA

SINTRA - MAFRA - CASCAIS

OBJECTO ANÓNIMO

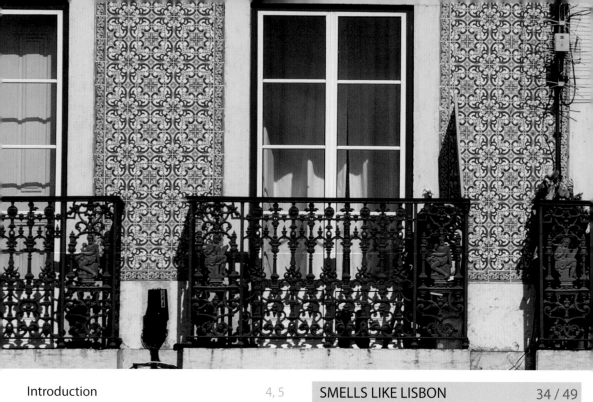

Introduction 4, 5

TRAVELLING BACK IN TIME 6 / 17

History of Lisbon 6, 7
Castelo de São Jorge 8, 9
Convento do Carmo 10
Sé de Lisboa 11
Museu Nacional de Arqueologia 12
Museu dos Coches 13
Palácio da Ajuda 14, 15
Museu Nacional de Arte Antiga 16, 17

NEW WORLDS TO THE WORLD 18 /33

The 'Age of Discovery' 20, 21
Torre de Belém 22, 23
Padrão dos Descobrimentos 24 / 27
Mosteiro dos Jerónimos 28 / 31
Museu da Marinha 32
Museu do Oriente 33

SMELLS LIKE LISBON 34 / 49

Baixa Pombalina 36, 37
Praça do Comércio 38, 39
Elevador de Santa Justa 40
Rua Augusta -41
Praça dos Restauradores 41
Praça D. Pedro IV (Rossio) 42, 43
Alfama 44, 47
Basílica da Estrela 48
Igreja de São Vicente de Fora 48
Casa dos Bicos 49
Panteão Nacional 49

A CITY FULL OF LIFE 50 / 65

Santo António 52
Santo António Weddings 52
Santo António – Lisbon Festivities 53 / 55
Traditional Market 56 / 59
Pastéis de Belém 60, 61
Feira da Ladra 62
Mercado da Ribeira 63
Lisbon Nights 64
Lisbon Theatres 65

MOMENTS OF INSPIRATION	66 / 81
History / Museu do Fado	68, 69
Amália Rodrigues	70, 71
Fado Singers / Fado Houses in Lisbon	72, 73
Lisbon Artists	74, 75
Fernando Pessoa	76, 77
Lisbon Cafés	78, 79
Fundação Calouste Gulbenkian	80, 81

ETERNAL LISBON	82 / 95
Ginjinha de Lisboa	86
Lisbon Kiosks	87
Lisbon Gardens	88, 89
Aqueduto das Águas Livres	90
Museu da Cidade	91
Museu Nacional do Azulejo	92, 93
Museu da Marioneta	94
Museu Bordalo Pinheiro	94
Museu de Arte Popular	95

LISBON TODAY	96 / 111
Parque das Nações	98 / 101
Cristo Rei	102
Ponte 25 de Abril	102, 103
Museu do Design e da Moda	104, 105
Museu Colecção Berardo	106, 107
Museu do Chiado	108
Urban Art	109
Jardim Zoológico	110, 111

BEYOND LISBON	112 / 127
Beaches Within the Lisbon District	114, 115
Palácio Nacional de Mafra	116
Palácio Nacional de Sintra	117
Palácio da Pena	118, 119
Castelo dos Mouros	120
Palácio de Monserrate	121
Sintra / Quinta da Regaleira	122, 123
Palácio de Queluz	124, 125
Cascais - Marina	126
Casa das Histórias Paula Rego	126, 127

| Credits | 128 |

Introduction

This book, this "trip" through Lisbon, was born from a desire to speak for the city and unravel its emotionally charged mysteries. Lisbon is a destination that welcomes us to its warm arms of golden houses and sloping streets. Each trail followed breathes and has countless stories to tell.

We've monitored the pulse of the city and we now unveil Lisbon through photographs, descriptions of places to visit, and a set of fictional stories.

We started this venture with the glorious "Age of Discoveries", a past stained with bloodshed, suffering and victory. One that brought forth the Portuguese as beings that had placed themselves above the gods; a story sung by the pen of poet - Luís de Camões. We continue such iniciative of "bringing new worlds to the world" through our outlook.

We invite you to let yourself be invaded by fragrances, those of Praça do Comércio (Commerce Square), streets lined by traditional shops, and the home of the Belém pastry known as 'Pastel de Belém' so as to discover some of Lisbon's fragrant essence.

The sun and moon also visit the city and grace it with two distinct views so to speak. By day we are taken to the Sights to behold one of them, and later, as night comes slowly through the streets giving off a glow, announcing a time for rest or enticing one to visit a Fado house. One sees a Lisbon that thrives, teeming with festivities such as that of Santo António (St. Anthony), with the joy felt at bars in the Bairro Alto, in theatres, and in museums.

Next we reveal the moments of inspiration that have germinated in the souls of poets, Fado singers, artists of all disciplines who have filled the city with moments of beauty and longing.

As always, Lisbon is a city that allows us to stroll through its gardens, look for refreshment at a traditional kiosk, or even find its story told in the Museu da Cidade (City's Museum).

Before ending the voyage we offer you a city tour of the city today which shows a route through the Parque das Nações (Park of Nations) and museums of contemporary art. We will reveal to you an urban art form that hides gray spaces with colour and messages of truth.

Finally, upon straying a bit from Lisbon, we suggest to you some places very close to the capital and worthy of a visit. You'll see Mafra, Sintra, Cascais and Queluz, promenade around the Cabo da Roca and beaches at Ericeira, Costa da Caparica and Maçãs (Sintra).

Lisbon is thus laid bare before your eyes through stories we offer with open arms in hopes that you make this trip with us. A trip through the sheets of this book and the city's illuminated streets.

SYMBOL OF THE CITY

Lisbon is the capital city of Portugal. It is located at the mouth and on the banks of the Tagus. It is the westernmost capital in Europe. This municipality covers an area of 84km² and its resident population is 556,797. It is the political, economic and cultural centre.

The greater Lisbon occupies approximately 2,750 km² and the 2.1 million people that commute to the capital make it very cosmopolitan. The old town stands on its seven hills: Estrela, Santa Catarina, São Pedro de Alcântara, São Jorge, Graça, Senhora do Monte and Penha de França. The western part of the city contains the Monsanto Forest Park. Lisbon at first began to extend and grow from the castle's hill. Phoenicians, Greeks and Carthaginians were attracted to this site due to a mild climate, abundance of flora and fauna, in addition to the river's valleys and hills. Later on came Romans who in turn exploited its port and fishing potential. They built several buildings such as temples, baths, palaces and a theatre.

Later occupation by barbarian tribes Alani, Swabians and Visigoths brought decline. During the Muslim occupation (719 - 1147) the city prospered once again. The Moorish Wall was constructed in addition to new neighbourhoods of narrow streets and alleys, creating a labyrinth that still exists in the Alfama quarter.

In 1147, the city was conquered by King Afonso Henriques. Court was later set up and strengthened the role of urban Lisbon as capital of the Kingdom (1256). The resulting population growth brought about the emergence of large housing units in areas outside the fortified walls, thus the constructing of the New (or Fernandina) Wall. Predominant places in the city in medieval times were: religious buildings, conventual squares and Rossio. The Portuguese 'Age of Discoveries' transformed the city into the commercial centre of Europe in the sixteenth century. The city's riverside was extensively modified due to the construction of buildings connected to the spice trade. The new public square next to the palace became a political and commercial centre. Sprouting along the riverside were: the Casa dos Bicos (House of Spikes), Madre de Deus Convent, the Jerónimos (Hieronymites) Monastery and Torre de Belém (Belém Tower). Planned for sailors and artisans, also at this time was the constructing of the Bairro Alto quarter.

In the 17th century – King João V – used gold from

OLD LISBON

1755 EARTHQUAKE

Brazil to make Lisbon a magnificent, pompous city. At this time, ensuring the city's water supply was built a great work – the Aqueduto das Águas Livres (Águas Livres Aqueduct).

The 1755 earthquake was devastating to the city, having destroyed its more populated areas. This was the darkest moment in the history of Lisbon. The earthquake also caused a Tidal Wave (tsunami) that swept thousands of people, boats and destroyed buildings. To top things off the city found itself beset by a devastating fire that lasted roughly three days.

Reconstruction of 'Pombaline' Downtown followed a visionary plan by the Marquis of Pombal.

The Rossio Square presently contains the oldest cafes, theatres and restaurants. Commerce Square lined with its arches and triumphal arch became one of the most beautiful squares in the world.

19th century liberalism established a new way of peceiving society. The most significant places thus became the city's Baixa (Downtown) and the Chiado – where plenty of shops, tobacco stores, cafes, bookstores, clubs and theatres could be found.

During the Estado Novo Regime (1926 - 1974) new housing districts and public buildings were built. The area in and around Belém changed and the bridge over the Tagus was inaugurated.

The years that followed the Revolution of April – 1974 were euphoric, and a time for modernization.

In the 90's the rehabilitation of historic districts began. Cultural and architectural heritage were valued.

EXPO 1998 spurred rehabilitation of the waterfront and in that year the construction of the Vasco da Gama bridge was completed. Lisbon's emblem is rooted in legend, history and myth. Dating back to the Middle Ages, it emerges from the Legend of St. Vincent's Martyrdom whose relics have always been accompanied by two ravens.

CASTLE OF SÃO JORGE

The **Castelo de São Jorge** (Castle of São Jorge) is a National Monument of historical, archaeological and architectonical importance. The castle exists since the 11th century, a time when Lisbon was a major Muslim seaport. In 1147, the first king of Portugal Afonso Henriques, conquered the castle and the city from the Moors.

From the 12th century to the beginning of the 16th century, the castle was a Royal Palace which received illustrious men, such as Gil Vicente , a great play-writer who presented at this place his first play. Life in the Court turned the castle into a privileged place, where King Manuel welcomed Vasco da Gama on his return from India.

The transfer of the royal residence to downtown and the earthquake of 1755 marked the decay of the castle which was subject to restoration works in the 20th century that conferred it the present importance and recovered its priceless historical value.

Today, on the eastern part of the castle named Praça Nova lies the Archaeological Centre, where remains from most ancient occupation of the area can be found and which date from the 7th century BC. The Museum at the Castle shows a collection of objects which allow the visitor to discover multiple cultures and experiences which helped to build the Lisbon we know today. The Periscope – the Tower of Ulysses – is situated in one of the castle´s towers and allows a panoramic view of the city of 360 – degree, in real time.

Standing on the highest hill of the historical centre, the castle offers its visitors one of the nicest views over the city and the Tagus estuary.

CASTLE OF SÃO JORGE LANDSCAPE →

CARMO CONVENT (INTERIOR)

CARMO CONVENT

CARMO CONVENT (DETAIL)

Built by the Carmelite Order and founded by D. Nuno Álvares Cabral in 1389, the **Convento do Carmo** (Carmo Convent) is located in the city's square called 'Largo do Carmo' on the hill opposite to Castle of São Jorge.

The temple being one of the largest and oldest in Lisbon, dating back from the Late Gothic era, was turned to ruins due to the city's massive 1755 earthquake and the devastating, ensueing fire.

That which remains of church's nave's ceiling disappeared with the quake leaving us only with the Gothic pointed arches that supported it.

The convent remains to this day as one of the last major remnants of the calamity that hit the city in 1755. Presently theses ruins are home to a Museu Arqueológico do Carmo (Archaeological Museum), housing artifacts dating from Pre-historic times onward. Noteable among these are Gothic tombs, Roman and Visigoth objects, and two Peruvian mummies.

Many visitors are attracted by the ruin's idyllic settings, where time seems at a standstill and upon which one can still sense that fatal, catastrophic date.

Originally called Igreja de St. Maria Maior (The Patriarchal Cathedral of St. Mary Major), in 1150 King Afonso I of Portugal ordered the constructing of the **Sé de Lisboa** (Lisbon Cathedral), an edifice that clearly takes its inspiration from the Old Cathedral of Coimbra's Romanesque style architecture.

Nevertheless in the present day it shows a mix of styles due to successive modifications and restorations over the centuries. The cathedral underwent transformation such as the construction of the Bartolomeu Joanes Chapel and the King Dinis cloister, both serving to exemplify Gothic, Portuguese cloisters; and the new main chapel plus an ambulatory built by King Afonso IV was added. The Franciscan chapel contains the sink where St. António was baptized in 1195 and is decorated with tiles showing the saint preaching to fish. In the adjacent chapel, there is a Baroque nativity scene made from cork, wood and terracotta by Machado de Castro.

The façade and the magnificent rose window in stained glass maintain their Romanesque appearance. The interior is dark for the most part, it is simple and austere. The Gothic cloister contains dainty double arches with beautiful carved capitals. One of the chapels has a thirteenth century iron wrought gate. Excavation within the cloisters has left important Roman remains out in the open for all to see.

LISBON CATHEDRAL

GALLERY

ATHENIAN PANATENAICA AMPHORA

The **Museu Nacional de Arqueologia** (National Archaeological Museum), founded in 1893 by Dr. José Leite de Vasconcelos, holds an ethnographic collection of significant size. It is a valuable collection that reflects the nations vast archaeological wealth. In addition to ceramics, sculpture, mosaics and glass, the museum is the residence of a priceless collection of archaic jewelery ranging from The Bronze Age to The Iron Age. The museum is located in the western wing of the Mosteiro dos Jerónimos (Hieronymites Monastery) where the former monks' dormitory used to be located. Permanent exhibitions at the museum are called: "Tesouros da Arqueologia Portuguesa", and "Antiguidades Egípcias" ('Portuguese Archaeological Treasures' and 'Egyptian Antiquity' – respectively). Aside from said exhibitions one can also visit temporary exhibits as well. The Museum offers other services: publication of books, conservation and restoration of archaeological objects, and educational services. It also has a specialized library, bookstore, and shop.

PHARAONIC BUST (7TH CENTURY – BC)

NATIONAL COACH MUSEUM

POPE CLEMENTE XI EMBASSY COACH

The **Museu Nacional dos Coches** (National Coach Museum), was created on the initiative of Queen D. Amélia whom had in turn christened it under the name Museu dos Coches Reais. However, with the fall of Portuguese monarchy and the nation turning into a Republic, the name was later changed to its current designation. The coaches therein where manufactured in Portugal, Italy, France, Austria and Spain, and are quite diverse in nature, some being simple yet others sophisticated. Today the museum along with its collection is considered unique in the world due to the variety in artistry borne by these handsome, ceremonial modes of transport that date back to the 17th, 18th and 19th centuries as well as due to the sheer number of displayable vehicles. Among vehicles displayed are Coaches, Wagons, Berlin Coaches, Carriages, Chariots, Buggies and Strollers. All are part of a distinct set allowing the visitor to apprehend the artistic and technical evolution within transportation methods for European courts thenceforth up to the appearance of the automobile.

PALACE FAÇADE

Comissioned by King José I to be built on one of the city's seven hills (Ajuda), the **Palácio Nacional da Ajuda** (Ajuda National Palace) is now a National Monument.

Built out of wood to better withstand earthquakes it was also known as 'The Wooden Court' or 'The Royal Shanty'. The decision to build in Belém/Ajuda was on account of the area's low seismic activity, and the Royal Family's having survived the 1755 quake that had layed to rubble their royal home.

In 1794, during the reign of Queen Maria I, a devastating fire completely ravaged the building alongwith much of its priceless possessions. A new plan was drawn up to rebuild the palace out of stone and mortar at the time but due to various factors the project was dropped.

The plan for reconstruction was placed into action when King Luís I came to the throne and the official site for the Royal Family's residence was chosen. From that moment on the location became synonymous with State affairs, council meetings, balls, and royal daily routine. The palace was closed down in 1910 with the onset of the Republic. Upon being openned to public view in 1968

people became capable of seeing the surroundings and collections pertaining to a royal family at the end of the nineteenth century. Based on rigorous historical research several rooms were restored. It is presently one of the most important museums for the Decorative Arts in the country, and is the setting for official state ceremonies. The areas of the palace open to public visitation include two floors, one being the ground floor where we can see chambers of a more private nature: The Music Room, The Blue Drawing Room, Dining Room, The Marble Room, and on the other floor holding highest significance for state affairs, the Piano nobile, where one can view spaces such as the Throne Room, and the grand Dining Room for events (State Banquets and Balls). The Palace also promotes other activities such as lectures, displays, courses and thematic visits.

PAGE 15→

01- QUEEN'S ROOM

02- THE DIPLOMATIC CORPS HALL

SCREEN NAMBAN (XVII CENTURY)

(THE TEMPTATION OF ST. ANTHONY), HIERONYMUS BOSCH

THE SAINT VICENT POLYPTYCH

The **Museu Nacional de Arte Antiga** (National Museum of Ancient Art) also known as "The Green Window Museum", is presently housed in a 17th century palace originally built for the Counts of Alvor. The museum's origin dates back to the Retrospective Exhibition of Ornamental Portuguese and Spanish Art held in 1882, in the halls of the "Palace Alvor-Pombal". The success of said event led to the purchase of the building by the State which in turn officially openned the National Museum of Fine Arts and Archaeology, two years later. In 1983 it was an integral part of the European Council Exhibition, and in 2006 it recieved Dr. Gustav Rau's collection "Fra Angelico to Bonnard". This collection's importance resides in the fact of it's being the most significant collection of Portuguese art between the fourteenth and nineteenth centuries. Among items most remarkable therein are: Painéis de S. Vincente panels (the Saint Vicent Polyptych) - a polyptych consisting of six panels painted in the 1460s, and the famous Hieronymus Bosch triptych - Tentações de Santo Antão (The Temptation of St. Antão).

BELÉM MONSTRANCE

New Worlds to the World

Within a house with a golden tiled façade lived a family that argued as much as they smiled. It was the home of a family like that of many others where the walls enclosed stories unseen by the outside world. As neighbours noticed, they traveled frequently. At certain times of year the girl would come knocking at the door asking to take care of the kitten while they were absent.

Their taste for travel was the subject of curiosity and musings regarding possible destinations, but the neighbours did not know of the existence of a deeper secret, one much more inspiring them to gossip about. According to the family patriarch who never tired in repeating the story to the remainder of those who dwelled in the home, the blood that ran in their veins was of an anonymous sailor. They were the descendants of a man who had taken part in the Age of Discoveries and had embarked on the famous voyage along with with Pedro Álvares Cabral in which land "Terras de Vera Cruz" (Brazil) was found.

There, to certify the veracity of the narrative was a string of beads that an Amerindian gave the anonymous sailor in exchange for a black sombrero. The string of beads prominently rested atop the fireplace's mantle. The patriarch would explain that each bead represented a world to discover, worlds of paradise, gods, and of heaven and hell. With the knowledge of this truth now residing within each of them, they would make trips without ever leaving home. For this reason all felt the desire to break the boundaries of knowledge without fearing the unknown, as in the past the anonymous sailor had done. The link to that glorious past was not only in their taste for adventure and travel, but mainly on their ability to reinvent themselves in a world of infinite possibilities.

This text is devoted to those anonymous. Those whose courage inspired the writing of this book.

Susana Fonseca

PORTUGUESE MAP OF EXPLORATIONS | → (TOP) BELÉM TOWER | → (DOWN) MURAL

It is difficult today, imbued with the concept of the "global village", a ready understanding of reality in which European communication with other continents was still far from 'flying' or of sending an 'instant' message.

Up to the 16th century, Europe maintained its ties with the known world through merchants for the most part - particularly Muslims - who, from far-flung territories of Africa or the confines of Asia brought the precious metals, silks and spices. In the opposite direction, the Crusades led many Europeans to the Middle East. Through these contacts exchanges between civilizations took place at what today would seem an unthinkable pace. At the turn of the 15th century Portugal was a kingdom depleted in resources though independent and at peace. War with Castile had worsened social and economic problems aggravated by the lack of grain and gold. The uprising of the bourgeoisie required the opening of new markets and nobility wanted to accomplish feats that would bring them prestige, power and wealth.

Thwarted by powerful Castile to increase territory in the Iberian Peninsula to expand the Portuguese were left with the open seas. It was in this context that in 1415, King João I along with his eldest children – Princes Duarte, Pedro and Henrique - left Lisbon; leading a strong Armada bound for North Africa thus conquering Ceuta. After losing Ceuta, the North Africans diverted gold and spice routes to other cities. It thus became necessary to discover the places of origin of those products that seemed to abound in Muslim Commerce. This need, coupled with the adventurous, brave and determined spirits of the Portuguese, caused them to thus set forth into the unknown to find and bring New Worlds to the world.

← PAGES. 18/19. HIERONYMITES MONASTERY

The **Torre de Belém** (Belém Tower) protrudes from the waters of the Tagus and is located where Belém beach used to be.

Built in the 16th Century it was part of the the Tagus estuary defensive plan that would protect the city (then the capital of a vast maritime empire) from piracy attacks or possible attacks of enemy nations.

With the development of other means for attack and defense, this structure lost its original function and was thenceforth used over the centuries for other purposes such as customs registration, telegraphy and as being a lighthouse. Its bunkers were used as dungeons for holding political prisoners.

This fortification has a bulwark and a square tower. Its shape is reminiscent of the towers within medieval castles. Much of its beauty comes from exterior details in Manueline style decor. One can see carved in stone: rope and tied knots, animal and plant motifs, religious statuary, open galleries, guard towers and battlements in the Moorish - shield-shaped – style. Quite unusual in other constructions of the gender this is a wonderful building. It blends all the requirements of military engineering with aesthetic care.

It is one of Lisbon's most expressive and symbolic monuments, classified by UNESCO as World Cultural Heritage for all Humanity.

BELÉM TOWER

The **Padrão dos Descobrimentos** (monument to the Age of Discoveries) was inaugurated in Belém in 1960 and was a strong presence in the memorial celebrations for the 500 years since the death of Prince D. Henrique the Navigator, the great patron of early European exploration. The sculpted composition consists of 33 figures connected to the Age of Discoveries, with Prince Henrique at the bow. Access to the monument is decorated with a wind rose and world map, where one can see all the routes of Portuguese Exploration. This decoration executed in marble was offered by the Republic of South Africa. People can visit the look-out at the top, the auditorium and two showrooms.

The panorama from the viewpoint is impressive, with all the beauty of the River Tagus to one side and the majestic Hieronymites Monastery to the other.

1 - INFANTE D.PEDRO (son of João I)
2 - D. FILIPA DE LENCASTRE (Mother of Prince D. Henrique)
3 - FERNÃO MENDES PINTO (Writer)
4 - FREI GONÇALO DE CARVALHO (Dominican)
5 - FREI HENRIQUE CARVALHO (Franciscan)
6 - LUÍS VAZ DE CAMÕES (Poet)
7 - NUNO GONÇALVES (Painter)
8 - GOMES EANES DE ZURARA (Chronicler)
9 - PERO DA COVILHÃ (Traveller)
10 - JÁCOME DE MAIORCA (Cosmographist)
11 - PÊRO DE ESCOBAR (Pilot)
12 - PEDRO NUNES (Mathematician)
13 - PÊRO DE ALENQUER (Pilot)
14 - GIL EANES (Navigator)
15 - JOÃO GONÇALVES ZARCO (Navigator)
16 - INFANTE D. FERNANDO (son of João I)
17 - INFANTE D. HENRIQUE (The Navigator – son of João I)

18 - D. AFONSO V (King)
19 - VASCO DA GAMA (Navigator)
20 - AFONSO BALDAIA (Navigator)
21 - PEDRO ÁLVARES CABRAL (Navigator)
22 - FERNÃO DE MAGALHÃES (Navigator)
23 - NICOLAU COELHO (Navigator)
24 - GASPAR CÔRTE REAL (Navigator)
25 - MARTIM AFONSO DE SOUSA (Navigator)
26 - JOÃO DE BARROS (Writer)
27 - ESTEVÃO DA GAMA (Captain)
28 - BARTOLOMEU DIAS (Navigator)
29 - DIOGO CÃO (Navigator)
30 - ANTÓNIO ABREU (Navigator)
31 - AFONSO DE ALBUQUERQUE (Governor)
32 - FRANCISCO XAVIER (Evangelist)
33 - CRISTOVÃO DA GAMA (Captain)

Infante D. Henrique (1394 - 1460), the 'Navigator', became the symbol and catalyst for the will and effort of all who set forth facing the unknown participating in the Age of Discovery. In 1415 he and his father (João I) headed a strong Armada and conquered Ceuta. He was left in charge to govern the city and that same year he was knighted.

According to description by chronicler Gomes Eanes de Zurara, the prince performed 'great deeds', devoted himself to hard work and was a man of 'brilliant advice and authority'. To him History owes the reconnaissance and settlement of the Atlantic islands. It was also the Prince who encouraged his squire Gil Eanes to sail beyond Cape Bojador, something hitherto thought not to be feasible on account of folk tales excluding the possibility of human life upon uncharted seas.

Also due to Prince Henrique's action sailors, mapmakers, manufacturers of nautical instruments and astrologers convened in Portugal. It was he who organized and planned the trips. It was thanks to his adventurous, encouraging spirit that the Portuguese gave Man a new world perspective.

Luís Vaz de Camões was an extraordinary poet and is one of the most important authors of the Portuguese language. He is believed to have been born in Lisbon either in 1517 or 1524 and most likely of noble gentry, giving him access to the court. It is also believed that he compiled studies due to the vast body of knowledge demonstrated in his work. He would have attended university around 1540. We know that he as a squire participated in a military expedition to North Africa and in Ceuta lost his right eye in combat. Shortly after 1550 he was in Lisbon and frequented the season's nobility and some ladies of court. At the time he led a bohemian life which ultimately led to his imprisonment. In 1553 he was released on the condition of going to the Orient. He went to India, Macao, and was shipwrecked - having lost all his property, saving himself by swimming, holding onto the manuscript of The Lusiads. Upon returning to Portugal in 1569 he prepared the publication of The Lusiads (1572), an epic poem dedicated to King Sebastião, who granted him an annual sum irregularly paid. In addition to his epic poem, Camões is the author of a vast lyrical body of work. Tradition has it that his last years were spent in misery, and that the poet had died a pauper on June 10th, 1580. The Lusíadas is the Portuguese epic par excellence because of its grandeur and universality. The book tells the story of Vasco da Gama and the Portuguese heroes. Camões brought renewal to the Portuguese language and is today one of the strongest symbols of his homeland's identity and of the Portuguese community.

Vasco da Gama played a major role in Portuguese history for having captained the first Armada to reach India. The date upon which was born this navigator and explorer of sea and land, hitherto unknown to Europeans, is unknown. The most likely dates lie between 1460 and 1469.

King Manuel I chose him to command four vessels (ships: St. Gabriel, St. Raphael, Berrio caravel, and a supply ship) with aims of reaching the riches of the East.

July 8 - 1497, Vasco da Gama and his crew sailed from the Tagus. Roughly after a year, after facing several dangers, the fleet finally reached India. The description of wealth given by Vasco da Gama regarding the kingdom of Portugal to the king of Calicut did not match the meager offering that he had brought (hats, sugar, olive oil, honey, etc.). The Zamorin was not overly impressed. This in the addition to intrigue woven by Arab merchants hindered the first contact between the two peoples. In August 1498, after repairing boats on the island of Angediva, Vasco da Gama began his return trip but it was only in the summer of 1499 that the vessel St. Gabriel sailed again in the nostalgic waters of the Tagus. Victims of shipwreck, disease and ambushes, about 2/3 of the crew did not return, including Vasco da Gama's own brother Paulo da Gama. The Cape Sea Route was thus established for making future trips to the East easier. Vasco da Gama was rewarded and recognized for this achievement. He led two more expeditions to India in order to enforce Portuguese interests in the East; in 1502 and in 1524, the year he died in Cochin victim to malaria.

ship carrying Brazilian wood, parrots and macaws was sent back to the king with the news. Cabral then set forth on his predetermined route, but a sudden storm in the South Atlantic sunk some ships. The fleet arrived in Calicut in September - 1500 with only six ships. A fortification was installed but was short-lived due to attacks by Muslims. Cabral then headed to Cochin and Cannanore where he loaded ships with spices and local produce, to later return to Portugal in 1501 and be hailed as a hero.

the country's inland by river. On this perilous journey the first contacts were made with the kingdom of Congo.

In 1485, on his second trip, Diogo Cão moved further south and realized that he had not reached the southern tip of Africa (Cape of Good Hope) as he had initially announced when reaching the mouth of the river Zaire.

Pedro Álvares Cabral was a nobleman in the court of King João II, and a Portuguese navigator. He was commander in the second maritime voyage to India. On this voyage, in 1500, Brazil was discovered.

He studied literature, history, science (cosmography), and the military arts. In 1499 he was appointed Captain of the fleet that would go to India upon the return of Vasco da Gama. Cabral's official mission was to establish diplomatic and trade relations with the Zamorin. To impress the king of Calicut his fleet was the best equipped in the fifteenth century, consisting of 13 ships and carrying roughly 1500 men. He left on March 8, 1500.

On April 22 - 1500, having drifted from the African coast, the fleet sighted land. Some say it was by accident, others say that Cabral was strictly following the King's secret plans. What is known for certain is that they landed in Brazil - namely Terra de Vera Cruz, and stayed there for a week. A

Diogo Cão made two trips in 1482 and 1486 where he explored the African coast from the Cape of Catarina to Serra Parda leaving markers (stone crosses with coat of arms), Padrões, along the way in places he deemed important for one reason or another during his voyages. On the first of the two expeditions, arriving at the mouth of Zaire, Diogo Cão ordered the exploration of

Bartolomeu Dias, was a navigator in the time of King João II and King Manuel I, but little is known of his biography. Bartolomeu Dias became famous for having passed the Cape of Good Hope, a journey undertaken in 1487-1488. He through his navigations demonstrated that the Atlantic and Indian Oceans communicated. The activity of this great navigator is unknown. We only know that by 1494 he became squire to the royal family and that he would some time later be endowed with the Guinea Warehouse. In 1500 he was chosen to captain one of the ships of Pedro Álvares Cabral's fleet bound for India, but was tragically wrecked in the same place that gave him fame upon passing the Cape of Good Hope.

SOUTH GATE

Mosteiro dos Jerónimos (Hieronymites Monastery), built in the late Gothic style of architecture known as "Manueline", is located in Belém. It replaced a small chapel founded by Prince Henry (Infante D. Henrique) where monks from the Order of Christ gave assistance to sailors. King Manuel (Dom Manuel) built it so as to make a pantheon for the members of his dynasty, dedicating the edifice to the Virgin of Belém (Virgin of "Bethlehem"). Construction began by 1501 and was finished a century later. The king (D. Manuel) channeled large sums, from revenues of trade with Africa and the East, for the endeavour. Much of said money came from profits from the spice trade, the so called 'Pepper Route'. To occupy the monastery king Manuel chose monks belonging to the Order of St. Jerónimo. Their main function was to pray for the the King's soul and salvation, as well as providing spiritual support for sailors and navigators that would set forth from the "Restelo Beach" with hopes of discovering more of the New World. Connected thus at the earliest stages in its life to the epic "Age of Discoveries", the monastery has practically always been associated to and held as being a symbol of the nation. During the nineteenth century it underwent various expansions and renovations giving it its present day look. Today the monument lets the viewer behold a blend of different styles: Renaissance, late Gothic and Manueline. Notable is the cloister and the South Gate of complex geometric design facing the Tagus River. The decorative elements are full of symbols of Nautical art along with sculptures of exotic plants and animals. The monument is considered World Heritage by UNESCO and on July 7th - 2007 it was elected as being one of the country's 'Seven Wonders'. Within it are tombs of some monarchs: Manuel I of Portugal, his wife Queen Maria, João III of Portugal, his wife Queen Catarina, D. Sebastião, D. Henrique, as well as the tombs of Vasco da Gama, Luís Vaz de Camões, Alexandre Herculano, and Fernando Pessoa.

FULL VIEW OF THE HIERONYMITES MONASTERY FAÇADE

19TH–20TH CENTURY HALL

A BATALHA NAVAL DO CABO MATAPAN (PAINTING DETAIL)

17TH–18TH CENTURY HALL

THE ROYAL BRIGANTINE

CHAMBER OF THE "AMÉLIA" ROYAL YACHT

Also in Belém is the **Museu de Marinha** (Naval Museum), located in the monastery's west wing.

The museum dates back to 1863 when King Luís proceeded to organize a collection regarding Portuguese maritime activities. Today the Museum is viewed as the Office for Cultural affairs for the "Portuguese War Navy" (also known as Portuguese Armada). Today, their mission is not only confined to naval military affairs, it is concerned first and foremost in the promotion of Portuguese maritime past along with everything that relates to the various aspects and activities of Man at sea.

The Naval Museum is comprised of several thematically organized areas. This way one can behold the diversity of vessels existent during 'The Age of Discovery' (also known as the "Age of Exploration" - Descobrimentos) that varied from tall eighteenth-century ships and ships of mixed propulsion from the nineteenth century, to the latest Portuguese 'Armada' Naval vessels. One can also see other types of craft such as those intended for cod fishing. Also viewable are the rooms within the "D. Amélia" Royal Yacht and the Galley pavilion. Here one can find on display the Royal Brigantine, built in 1778, in Lisbon. Also therein is the seaplane that completed the first aerial crossing of the South Atlantic – the "Santa Cruz", a plane that in 1922 had been manned by naval officers Sacadura Cabral and Gago Coutinho. The museum also has a vast collection of weapons, uniforms, instruments and navigational charts. It holds temporary exhibits and offers trips upon the Tagus River in traditional boats.

← PÁGS. 30/31. HIERONYMITES MONASTERY

PERFORMANCE DRESS FOR THE BARONG, BALI, INDONESIA　　*VISHNU AND HIS MANY ENCARNATIONS, INDIA, 19TH CENTURY*　　*QIN QIONG, THE GOD OF DOORWAYS, CHINA, 19THCENTURY*

DRESS OF KARIMKUTTISHASTAN, TEYYAM CEREMONY, NABA PAUL, INDIA, KERALA, 19THCENTURY

The **Museu do Oriente** (Orient Museum) is housed in the old warehouses of Regulatory Commission for The Commerce of Cod, in Alcântara. The Museum is the responsibility of the "Oriente" Foundation and opened in 2008 with the task of baring witnesses to both the Portuguese presence in Asia, and to the different Asian cultures.

This is a museum that seeks to provide all visitors with a 'living' memory, of active Asian cultures and the secular relation that was established between East and West, mainly through Portugal. The museological heritage for the permanent exhibits of the Orient Museum is divided essentially into two main collections: the Portuguese Presence in Asia collection, and Kwok On Collection.

The art collection regarding the Portuguese presence in Asia has several pieces of exceptional value, especially several Chinese and Japanese screens from 17th and 18th centuries, various pieces of Namban art of great rarity, a collection of porcelain emblazoned pieces of Companhia das Índias and a significant collection related to the people in East Timor.

The Kwok On Collection encompasses all genres conveying myths and stories of cultures common to the great Asian civilizations. It also brings us: costumes, masks, musical instruments, accessories, theatre and shadow puppetry, for performance. These represent in Asia that which is at times more sacred in nature. The collection includes also paintings and engravings that illustrate not only myths and stories and the rituals of staging, but also anthropomorphic or symbolic representations of deities, statues, pictures, altars and celebrant accessories.

The Museum of the East is organized around two permanent exhibitions: Portuguese Presence in Asia and Gods in Asia. Simultaneously the museum presents a program of temporary exhibitions dedicated to the dissemination of the arts in Asia.

Smells Like Lisbon

*L*et us speak of joy - of feelings, odours and abstract ideas as we try to find the smells that float within and above the sloping landscapes of the city.

Let us look upon its terraces in the late afternoon where the soft sun bids 'adieu'. Now that summer has gone to a faraway place I already miss its warm conversations accompanied by cold drinks.

Are you familiar with the scent of saudade(longing)? Imagine a bouquet of red roses, a gift from that special someone, then hold the roses with care, close your eyes and draw from them their fragrant essence. Nostalgia smells like fresh roses. There is also the scent of autumn fun; the joy of having roasted chestnuts and of good news that arrives unexpectedly by mail, that smell that invades us with each cup of steaming hot chocolate. On the other hand melancholy seems to be ever-present, a sense of longing from the smell of wet leaves on the ground after a rainy day.

We then continue on our journey with the smell of adventure that transports us to crystal clear river waters; whereas the smell of hatred and betrayal leads me through dark alleys. In these lurks the scent of Fear bearing a sign of superiority. Yes Fear always thinks it's bigger than everyone but how many times is it cheated and caught by surprise when one walks alone?

Then we arrive to the scent of a city almost asleep, in peace. We thus arrive at our destination in the smell of a quiet glass of red wine.

Within the sense of love we come to the smell of freshly baked Belém pastries. You don't believe me? I'll take this further by saying that love soothes us with a scent of wild berries and that Fado (fate) enters through open windows and through the cracks of doors left ajar. Fado (fate) has several scents: some is of bush basil, others are of the bodies of people distressed by a shattered life. Let us talk of smells. The fragrances of a Lisbon that lives in peoples homes and that becomes books regarding "Truth". Each truth smells like a green apple. One takes a bite and it changes, taking upon itself new forms. Do you know where you can find the smell of poetry? I know it's hard to believe, but it can be found hanging in clothes that dry from windows.

Susana Fonseca

MARQUIS OF POMBAL

Sebastião José de Carvalho e Melo (1699 -1782) became known as the **Marquis of Pombal** and was appointed Minister to the Kingdom by King José I.

On November 1 - 1755 a violent earthquake devastated the lower districts of Lisbon. The Marquis of Pombal took immediate action: ordering the burying of the dead and aiding those wounded, ordering the surveillance of the city so as to prevent theft, and instructing a team of architects to make the plans for reconstruction. Thus it was that less than one year after the calamity, Lisbon had already been partially rebuilt.

The Marquis of Pombal himself accompanied the rebuilding of the city. He decided upon razing the lower area which had suffered most of the destructive force and built a newer broadened area now refered to as - Pombaline Lisbon. This style has its own characteristics: wide streets - perpendicular to each other, mosaic walks, sewers, harmonious buildings - all of same height with beautifully

← *PAGES 34/35.GRILLED SARDINES, ALFAMA*

TERREIRO DO PAÇO (COMMERCE SQUARE)

LISBON CITY HALL

wrought iron balconies and built with a protection system against earthquakes, and a large square – Praça do Comércio (Commerce Square) - situated in the old Palatial Square where the streets acessed the "noble" areas of the city. Such decision-making and effectiveness by the Marquis of Pombal permitted his gaining the trust and full support from the king. He then began a series of reforms (trade, education and industry) to develop the nation and to strengthen the king's absolute power (despotism). "Pombaline" Downtown Lisbon is now one of the city's tourist attractions.

BAIXA POMBALINA (DOWNTOWN)

COMMERCE SQUARE | → (UP) ARCHES/ STREETCAR | → (DOWN) KING JOSÉ Iˢᵀ SCULPTURE/PEDESTRIAN FEEDING PIDGEONS WITH CORN

Praça do Comércio (Commerce Square) is in downtown Lisbon and located next to the Tagus river in the area which used to be part of the palace of Portuguese kings for nearly two centuries. It is one of the largest squares in Europe. In 1511 King Manuel I moved his residence from the Castle of São Jorge to this location but the *Ribeira* (Riverside) Palace was totally razed following the 1755 earthquake.

In the reconstructing of downtown Lisbon the plaza became the core element the Marquis of Pombal's plan.

Buildings lined with arcades surrounding the square are now home to some departments of various ministries of the Portuguese government, and also the famous *Café Martinho da Arcada* - the oldest in Lisbon and one of Fernando Pessoa's favourites. The yellow tones on these buildings within this wide area facing the river offer visitors a journey somewhere between dreams and reality. In the center of the square one finds the statue of King José I, erected in 1775 by Machado de Castro. On the north side of the square is the Triumphal Arch of *Rua Augusta*. It is the entrance to the downtown district. This refurbished plaza also became part of Portugal's history through the 1908 regicide of King Carlos, and the revolt of the armed forces that overthrew the government in 1974. This square later had also served as a car park but today this vast space is used for cultural events and shows.

THE LIFT'S TOP FLOOR VIEWPOINT

The Unusual neogothic style monument also known as the "Carmo Lift", the **Elevador de Santa Justa** (Santa Justa lift), was built in the historic centre of Lisbon. The elevator links the streets Rua do Ouro and Rua do Carmo to the city's historic Carmo Square.

The structure was designed and built in iron with lacy embellishments by engineer Raoul Mesnier du Ponsard at the turn of the century (19th to 20th). In its early years the lift was steam-driven, only later did it come to be electrically powered. It was considered at the time as being a bold piece of work for various reasons: the overcoming of the steep slope, materials used, and the viaducts built that bridge the different levels thus permitting access to the upper part of the city's hill known as "Carmo". Passengers can climb or go down one of the lift's elaborate booths. The views from the top floor are magnificent and allow one to see the Rossio, Lisbon's downtown, the Castle of São Jorge, the Tagus river, and the ruins of the Carmo Convent Church.

THE LIFT SEEN FROM OURO STREET

AUGUSTA STREET ARCH

Rua Augusta is one of the most famous downtown Lisbon streets. It starts at the magnificent triumphal arch and connects the city's Commerce Square to Rossio. It is a street full of commercial activity, with a variety of shops and stores on both sides. Street artists, artisans and vendors are also part of this street's life, making it one of the city's most lively routes during the day.

The city's square known as **Praça dos Restauradores**, its name pertaining to the Restoration War, is located between Liberdade Avenue and King Pedro IV Square. It is a very busy area and the high obelisk within it celebrates the country's liberation from Spanish dominion in 1640. The bronze figures at the obelisk's base represent "Victory" and "Liberty". This public square provides access to the Glória walkway and lift.

ROSSIO TRAIN STATION

PORTUGUESE COBBLESTONE

Praça D. Pedro IV (King Pedro IV Square), better known as **Rossio**, is one of the busiest and most beautiful squares in Lisbon where thousands of people commute every day, most of them being on their way to a variety of destinations.

It was named after King Pedro IV due to there being in its centre an imposing statue of this Portuguese king (and first emperor of independent Brazil). At the base of the statue there are four female figures each representing Justice, Wisdom, Strength and Moderation; all being qualities attributed to the king. The Pombaline style buildings surrounding the Square are filled with souvenir shops, jewellery stores and cafés. Noteworthy among these cafés is the Café Nicola - a living tribute to the Portuguese poet, Bocage.

By the middle of the 19th century the square was paved in wavy patterns of black and white cobblestones. At the north side lies the beautiful National Theatre D. Maria II. Another magnificent edifice impossible to go unnoticed is the Rossio train station with its dazzling neo-Manueline style façade. An odd feature regarding its interior that now links to the Metro (Underground) is that the platforms are situated 30 metres above the main entrance. Amidst visitors and those that dwell in the city, filling the square's many cafés, Lisbon's true cosmopolitan pulse can be felt.

FOUNTAIN – D. PEDRO IV STATUE – D. MARIA II THEATRE

STREETS OF ALFAMA

Of Lisbon's various quarters, **Alfama** is one of the most typical. Everything here seems to come from the timeless power of memory: narrow streets, steep stairways, tile façades on houses, clothes lines, vases full of flowers, cats that creep in and onto balconies, neighbours who talk about the weather and the state of things, children running, and passing visitors who take pictures of glimpsing moments so as to later recollect.

Views from Alfama of the cityscape and Tagus River inspire and are a haven for thought. Viewpoints include: Portas do Sol, Santa Luzia, the São Jorge Castle, the Church of São Vicente de Fora, and the National Pantheon among other places. Amidst houses and courtyards one finds traces of Roman and Arabic occupation. The Lisbon Cathedral shows the passage of time and reflects a mix of architectural styles.

A home to sailors in the past, this quarter is also renown for having a variety of typical restaurants, traditional shops, antiquarians, and handcraft stores. During the Summer fests that celebrate the Saints, especially "Santo António", the streets teem with people, sardines and basil. Every morning Alfama awakens to the sound of streetcars and every night slumbers to the sound of guitars playing in Fado houses.

PAGE 45→ 01- VIEW OF ALFAMA / 02- STREETCAR

The **Basílica da Estrela** (Estrela Basilica*)* is located atop a hill on the west side of town. In the second half of the eighteenth century The Queen Maria I made the promise that she would build a convent if she had a son, this eventually happened. The temple bears the characteristics of the late baroque and neoclassical styles. Its inside covered in gray, pink and yellow marble - is large and its dome is lighted by apertures. The austere atmosphere within, and especially the Empire style tomb of Queen Maria, gives one a sense of solemnity.

ESTRELA BASILICA

MONASTERY OF SÃO VICENTE DE FORA

← *PÁGS. 46/47. VIEW OF ALFAMA*

Also known as the **Mosteiro de São Vicente Fora**, the Monastery of São Vicente de Fora is located in the historic Alfama district. In the same location king - D. Afonso Henriques had had a temple built also honouring São Vicente. Inside the church and notable are the impressive Baroque altar plus the eight life-size wooden images painted white. Accessible from the nave, the former adjacent Augustinian monastery has traces of the old cloister and is noteworthy also due to its eighteenth century, tile panels. Those most relevant are the ones that depict the La Fontaine fables. This monastery gives visitors an idea of the lifestyle led by the monks who had lived there. Atmosphere here is quiet and the view from the top is one of the best in town.

Casa dos Bicos (House of Spikes) or Brás de Albuquerque House was built in 1523 as a residential home. Making the building unique among the city's architecture are the diamond shaped stone spikes that appear upon its façade, thus revealing an Italian Renaissance style architecture.

Upon having its upper floors destroyed during the Great Lisbon Earthquake (1755) the Albuquerque family sold the residence.

It later came to be the commercial headquarters and deposit for Cod. The House was rebuilt in 1983 on account of the "17th Art, Science and Culture Exhibition". At present it houses the Saramago Foundation and the Nobel Prize laureate's library.

HOUSE OF SPIKES

The **Panteão Nacional** (National Pantheon) is located in the historic Santa Clara campus and occupies the building originally intended for the Church of Santa Engracia. The Pantheon houses the tombs and cenotaphs of some of the nation's great historic figures. Among said tombs one can find the famous fado singer Amália Rodrigues. The building is itself impressive with its remarkable dome, coloured marble, and its nave has ample space. As one climbs the stairs that lead up to the church, it is possible to have multiple perspectives of the building. There are various stopping points along the climb so one can enjoy the stunning views of the city.

NATIONAL PANTHEON

A City Full of Life

She woke up with a ring-tone of there being a message on her phone. Turning to the other side she almost continued to slumber but by impulse got up to look and check her messages. Suddenly all sleepiness left her as she became filled with energy and vitality. Running to the window and stroking the white cat that lounged about the house, her eyes settled on her Bush Basil. Her hands touched the blooming plant and the smell of bustle of the night before invaded her nostrils.

As in previous years she'd always gone out with her friends on the festive eve of St. António. Everywhere there was a hustle of people, colourful streets, grilled sardines and tents lined with Bush Basil and music that echoed toward the skies of a city in celebration. She had caught the tram to go see the festivities with her friends as she delighted in all the excitement and joy that surrounded her, remembering the basil that someone had left at her door two days before. Even after reading the Bush Basil's caption again and again, she still hadn't grasped its full meaning.

"within this bush
lies life ladden with
the scent of the sea
and a colour ridden verse
enticing you to dance"

It had been a memorable night and she lay there, exhausted after watching the parade of popular marches. She herself had danced until the dawn. Once awoken by the message on the phone she discovered that St. António Day that year would mark her life forever.

"Mary I've returned to Lisbon and shall leave to France no longer! Hope you enjoyed the basil :-) I've never forgotten you! Can we meet? "
Her childhood friend who had participated in marches alongside her had just returned from abroad and had come back to live in the city...

Susana Fonseca

BRIDES COMING OUT OF THE CHURCH

STAINED GLASS INSIDE THE CATHEDRAL (ST. ANTÓNIO)

BRIDES (ENTERING THE CHURCH)

Santo António - c. 1190 – 1231, who had been named Fernando Martins de Bulhões and Brother António upon admission into the Franciscan Order, was born in Lisbon. At first he entered the Augustinian Monastery "São Vicente de Fora" but it was in Coimbra that he first came into contact with Franciscans. Ideals such as: humility, poverty, evangelism and martyrdom drew him in. He made several trips and was known to be a great preacher, composing several Sermons to serve as models for Franciscan monks. He died in Pádua, Italy. In Portugal he has been worshiped from early on but it was through the celebrating of his day on the 13th of June and thus overlapping the celebrating of the Summer Solstice that he became one of the most popular saints in the country, especially in Lisbon where it is a municipal holiday. Festivities in honour of St. António reach a high point on the eve of June 12. There is a parade with popular marches that cascade down the avenue (Avenida da Liberdade). The event ends with major fireworks and a party that lasts into the evening with people celebrating in different neighbourhoods eating grilled sardines, pork steaks, soup (caldo verde) and drinking red wine.

The **Casamentos de Santo António** (Saint António Weddings) are a popular and traditional event of great significance to the city of Lisbon. It is an integral part of the city's identity and cultural heritage. Santo António is also known as the marriage saint. Legend has it that he was an excellent wedding councillor. For this reason each year on the 12th of June Lisbon City Hall holds and pays for the weddings of approximately 15 couples.

PAGE 53→

01- SELLING BASIL

02- GRILLING SARDINES

← *PÁGS. 50/51. LISBON POPULAR MARCHES*

LISBON POPULAR MARCHES

The St. António festivity is one of the best known and liveliest fests in Portugal.

The "popular marches" that take place at Avenida da Liberdade (avenue) began in 1932. It is a great night attraction. The avenue is thus filled with light, colour, dance, the rhythmic pace of the music (marches), and the joy of those participating in a unique festival in their town. Parading by civil parish, one can see the the result of the year's work. In hopes of being recognized by the jury and thus winning the contest each parish group comes forth with the lyrics, music and choreography for songs; dressing themselves accordingly based on each year's theme. Every year the parochial rivalries spur each neighbourhood to show its best. The jury ultimately casts its vote, and not always in agreement with the opinions of viewers and participants. With many public figures and municipal politicians, participating among them - the mayor. This event is broadcast by national television. Each neighbourhood invites a man and woman, usually acclaimed figures from the entertainment business to be their 'godfathers' for the night.

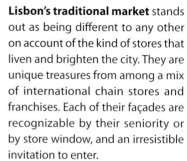

LORETO CANDLE HOUSE (LORETO STREET 53/55)

ULISSES GLOVE SHOP (CARMO STREET 87/A)

Lisbon's traditional market stands out as being different to any other on account of the kind of stores that liven and brighten the city. They are unique treasures from among a mix of international chain stores and franchises. Each of their façades are recognizable by their seniority or by store window, and an irresistible invitation to enter.

The store "Conserveira de Lisboa", located in the street "Rua dos Bacalhoeiros"is a stupendous example of the mentioned traditional market, it is a fish store. Various manually packed cans of fish line the walls of this store.

The "Ulisses" glove shop has been marking a difference in the street "Rua do Carmo"bearing the original decor from the time of its foundation.

To enter any of these traditional stores is an amazing experience.

CHIADO BERTRAND BOOKSTORE

Located in the heart of Lisbon, the **Livraria Bertrand do Chiado** (Chiado Bertrand Bookshop) is a place full of stories. The first Bertrand Bookshop was established in 1732, by Pedro Faure, at Rua Direita do Loreto. After the earthquake of 1755, it was settled next to the Capela de Nossa Senhora das Necessidades. Eighteen years later, it was moved to the newly rebuilt city centre, called "baixa pombalina" (downtown). Some famous Portuguese authors used to go there, such as Aquilino Ribeiro and Eça de Queirós.

In 2011, it was considered the oldest bookshop in the world by the Guinness World Records.

PAGE 57→ (from up to the right)

01- DOLL HOSPITAL (FIGUEIRA SQUARE, 7)

02- LISBON CANNERY (BACALHOEIROS STREET, 34)

03- A VIDA PORTUGUESA (ANCHIETA STREET,11)

04- ROSSIO HAT SHOP (ROSSIO SQUARE)

A CITY FULL OF LIFE

THE CARIOCA (MISERICÓRDIA STREET, 9)

BIJOU HABERDASHERY (CONCEIÇÃO STREET 91)

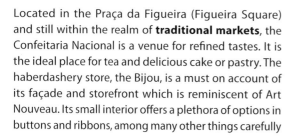

ALENTEJO HOUSE (PORTAS DE ST. ANTÃO STREET, 58)

Located in the Praça da Figueira (Figueira Square) and still within the realm of **traditional markets**, the Confeitaria Nacional is a venue for refined tastes. It is the ideal place for tea and delicious cake or pastry. The haberdashery store, the Bijou, is a must on account of its façade and storefront which is reminiscent of Art Nouveau. Its small interior offers a plethora of options in buttons and ribbons, among many other things carefully organized therein. In the Carioca one finds bags and cans full of Tea, packaged coffee, glass jars filled with coloured candy, and the unmistakable pleasant fragrance of fresh coffee. Within the impressive building, Casa do Alentejo, and among the arches of its Arabic courtyard there is a shop with traditional products from Alentejo - these being hand crafts, books and other publications.

CONFEITARIA NACIONAL (FIGUEIRA SQUARE 18B)

The shop known as **"A Casa dos Pastéis de Belém"** (to loosely translate from the Portuguese - House of Belém Pastries) is one of the busiest stores in town. Once we set foot inside we are overwhelmed by the scent of these pastries and instantly realize the reason being for so much hustle and bustle. The shop is always teaming with people entering and leaving, waiting for their turn at the counter, or sitting and partaking in the hot and sweet, unforgettable taste of these delectable pastries.

In 1837, in an attempt to raise funds the clergy from the monastery put these custard pastries on sale in a shop which eventually came to be known as "Pastéis de Belém". When the monastery closed the baker sold the recipe to a Portuguese businessman called Domingos Rafael Alves, and today it still continues to belong to his descendants. Since then approximately 10,000 of these pastries have been baked per day. The recipe is revealed to the master bakers who in turn bake them in the old fashioned way at the store's "Secret Shop". Upon consumption, served plain or doused with cinnamon and powdered sugar, this pastry brings us a flavour from the past, and we thus sense a taste of nostalgia.

PASTÉIS DE BELÉM

FEIRA DA LADRA

The flea market known as **Feira da Ladra** is a popular public fair that takes place on Tuesdays and Saturdays in the city's Santa Clara campus (within the civil parish of São Vicente de fora). In this market used objects are sold. At the fair there is a constant bustle of buyers that look into stands or upon the colourful cloths that lay on the ground bearing second-hand items.

Here one has a selection of books, magazines, paintings, furniture, scrap metal, vinyl, toys, electrical appliances and other even more curious objects to choose from. The buyer is indeed not indifferent to such an array.

INTERIOR OF THE MARKET

Mercado da Ribeira is a market located on the waterfront and next to "Cais do Sodré". The site dates back to the ancient Mercado da Ribeira Velha (Old River Market) which stood in front of the landmark "Casa dos Bicos". Today, Ribeira Market has reinvented itself and presents 31 eating spots and cultural attractions. The food on offer ranges from seafood to steak sandwiches, hamburgers and ice-cream. Among other products, visitors can buy meat, fresh vegetables and flowers.

MAIN FAÇADE

DOCKS AND "THE 25 ABRIL" BRIDGE

CLUB MAXIME

The **docks** are located next to the Tagus River. It is a place where old warehouses once stood. Currently this area has a wide variety of restaurants and bars with live music. Terraces also abound and the atmosphere is conducive to partying till the wee hours.

BAIRRO ALTO

Bairro Alto, a historic neighbourhood in Lisbon, becomes one of the most cosmopolitan and bohemian in the city by nightfall. Its streets are lined with bars, terraces, restaurants, fado houses, fashion shops, workshops, art galleries and other alternative spaces. For those looking for fun it is the ideal place for an evening out. In every street, there are different musical styles, thus a high supply of spots and for every taste.

SÃO CARLOS NATIONAL THEATRE

The **Teatro Nacional D. Maria II** (National Theatre D. Maria II) is located in the D. Pedro IV plaza (Rossio) and opened its doors to the public in 1846. Since then this theatre has been an integral part in the city's cultural life, politics and even its history. The theatre **A Comuna** – Teatro de Pesquisa is located in Praça de Espanha. The theatre was born under this name in 1972. The first show performed therein was based on works by the great playwright Gil Vicente.

The theatre **Politeama** came to being due to the dreams of a man passionate about the performing arts. Due to the wishes of Luis António Pereira it came to be in 1913 in the Rua das Portas de Santo Antão. Here the stage was shared by prestigious theatre groups. It is presently stage to famous musical performances by Filipe La Feria. The **Teatro Nacional São Carlos** (National São Carlos Theatre) is a magnificent, imposing edifice located at Rua Serpa Pinto. It has been part of the city's history and life since 1793.

Moments of
Inspiration

$\mathcal{P}$ortuguese poet Luís Vaz de Camões asked the Tágides (the Tagus river nymphs) to help him sing in a sublime fashion the feats of the Portuguese people, and it was by cunning wit and artistry that his epic is (and was read everywhere). Was the making of "The Lusiads", a work that stands alone based on real facts and translated into several languages, thoroughly analyzed in detail, simply the sum of moments of divine inspiration? Do the Tágides continue to bathe in the mysterious waters of the Tagus? We believe that the spirit of Camões lives therein. Fernando Pessoa who has left a legacy of poems and writings, whom unfolds through heteronyms and strolled the streets of Lisbon sprouting new ways of interpreting reality; wrote and spoke at cafés such as Martinho da Arcada and the Brasileira, continues to breathe in those reading, an oeuvre regarding a homeland never before seen, and torments never before felt. We believe that Fernando Pessoa continues to walk the streets and cafes of Lisbon, and that at night he sleeps in the house that bares his name.

Fado diva and a beautiful woman, Amália Rodrigues, who's "strange livelihood" (Estranha forma de vida) reflects the identity of the many, is herself the city - still breathing in its hills, viewpoints, Fado houses and sublime vocal chords of present day Fado singers. Amália was not just a pretty voice she was a presence complete and full to those who "read" her, yet being unto herself incomplete. The heart of Amália is still lost and among us. It continues to bleed a song of longing, love and emotion that escapes and surprises us from within.

Hip Hop singer Sam The Kid also uses Camões's tongue to sing about a "strange livelihood" that brings us a sensation we fail to understand. Perhaps these misconceptions are whispered to us by the Tágides, reaching those of more sensitive ears that in turn, turn it into art.

This is our reflection on the city, a place intangible. It is dedicated to all Lisbon artists who have put on paper, canvas; in a voice or the strings of a guitar, the emotions that move us and "wind" a train we call 'heart'. Thank you for your inspiration.

Susana Fonseca

"O FADO" BY JOSÉ MALHOA, 1910

Fado became popular back in 19th century Lisbon during moments of leisure and conviviality. It spontaneously became manifest in the streets, alleys, gardens, in the run of bulls, taverns and in cafés of chambermaids. Initially Fado was linked to a social context characterized by crime and transgression. Many sources evoke the involvement of aristocrats and Fado singing harlots. This is pictured and mentioned in many poems, sung in films, the theater, visual arts, and literature.

Revista type theatre included the singing of this music and thus making it reach a wider audience through renowned artists and Fado singers. The emergence of Fado companies allowed the promotion of professional performances and international tours. Gradually this music would be heard in Fado houses, places which would mainly be rooted within the city's historic neighbourhoods.

The **Fado Museum**, opened in 1998, is a museum devoted to the world of fado and guitar. It is located in the *Alfama* district. It is a cultural space with a permanent exhibition, a Documentation Centre, and a store among other spaces. It is entirely devoted to the world of Lisbon's urban musical genre. It celebrates the exceptional value of Fado as an identifying symbol of Lisbon.

← PAGES 66/67. FADO IN THE STREETCAR

LISTENING POST

"O MARINHEIRO" BY CONSTANTINO FERNANDES, 1913

PORTUGUESE GUITAR

PORTUGUESE FADO ARTISTS' PANEL

FADO MUSEUM PANEL

Amália da Piedade Rodrigues (Lisbon, 1920-1999) was a Portuguese singer, actress and Fado artist. Hailed worldwide as the voice of Portugal, she became internationally known as the Queen of Fado and considered among the best ambassadors of Portuguese culture through the symbolism of the musical genre she had sung. Through various television programs her voice was heard in many a home. In addition to fado, Amália also sang songs of Portuguese folk tradition, songs of the day and and even foreign pieces.

Her contribution to the history of fado was remarkable and in diverse respects: her unmistakable voice, performance practice, and the singing poems by great Portuguese authors after being set to music. Amalia lived in Lisbon and from an early age was left to the care of grandparents. Her musical talents were notable in early childhood when she would sing to her grandfather and neighbours. At the age of 9 Amália began to go to school, but at 12 had to interrupt her studies as was common in poor families. At 14 she moved in with her parents who had returned to Lisbon but her youth, having to work simultaneously as an embroiderer, ironing, and various other odd jobs was not an easy one. At 15, selling fruit, her voice would not go unnoticed. During the "Santo António" festivities she joined the Alcântara neighbourhood "Popular march". In 1940 she made her debut on stage with "Revista" type plays. In 1943 she performed for the 1st time outside of Portugal. The following year she had a major role next to Hermínia Silva in the "Rosa Cantadeira" operetta.

In September she went to Brazil to work at the Copacabana Casino. The show's reception was so enthusiastic that she was invited to extend her contract. She also recorded in several countries and aroused great interest in Hollywood. In 1947 she first appeared on film in "Capas Negras" which then became the most watched up to then in Portugal. In the same year she entered in the film "Fado, História de uma Cantadeira". Amália was loved by renown artists such as Almada Negreiros. The phenomenal, exponential internationalization of Amália emerged from her participation in Marshall Plan performances. The success of her songs was repeated in Trieste, Bern, Paris and Dublin. In Rome she performed at the Teatro Argentina. In 1952 she debuted in New York on the La Vie en Rose stage. The following year, she performed before cameras for NBC. In the U.S. her first album on vinyl 33 rpm was released. With the advent of democracy in Portugal great homage was paid to Amália who then received several awards both in Portugal and abroad. The value of this brilliant performer was and is recognized. In 1999 Amália died at home.

It was a quick death. Her remains ly in the National Pantheon among those of other illustrious Portuguese figures. Despite her death her musical legacy lives on. Inspirational to many Fado artists of the present day such as Carminho and Mariza. Her spirit shall eternally live on through projects such as "Amália Hoje" that try to live up to this diva.

MOMENTS OF INSPIRATION

ALFREDO MARCENEIRO

FERNANDO MARINHA

FERNANDO MAURÍCIO

CARLOS PAREDES

CARLOS DO CARMO

ARGENTINA SANTOS

MARIZA

KÁTIA GUERREIRO

CAMANÉ

MARIA DA FÉ

CARMINHO

ANA MOURA

What makes the musical genre into something unique that you can feel and hear in a special manner are the singers, other accompanying musicians who do so on the guitar, and the Fado houses themselves. Many are those who have along the ages sung and voiced the musical genre known as Fado.

Hermínia Silva became a central figure in the history of Fado and a consecrated stage star in the '30s and '40s. Amália Rodrigues brought prestige to the genre rendering it internationally famous. She thus gained the status of being a national cultural icon. With Amália Fado pushed beyond cultural and language frontiers.

Fernando Farinha was renowned for singing Fado in the '50s and '60s and one of the first fado singers to record and perform accompanied by an acoustic bass guitar.

A gifted master known for his improvisation and the (Desgarrada) "Duelling Fado", Alfredo Merceneiro was an artist who marked the history of fado profoundly. Throughout a career spanning nearly 60 years he revealed a unique way of singing, placing emphasis on lyrics. More recently artists have been in attendance with greater

regularity on international stages. Fado became a form of World Music that has gained more and more importance worldwide, it can more readily be found. Fado has gone global, and some work has been under the influence of other musical areas such as jazz, classical music, electronic music and "ethnic" genres coming from other parts of the world. Camané is one of the leading male voices of this new generation and often acts abroad.

Throughout her career Mariza has won audiences with her vocal power, her unique "soulful"sound, discipline and work. She is now considered one of the great vocal artists, alongside Amália, Edith Piaf, Ellis and other outstanding divas. Other artists such as Ana Moura, Mafalda Arnauth, Kátia Guerreiro and Ricardo Ribeiro have currently been prominent.

Within the **Fado Museum** one can see the evolution of fado throughout its existence as well as the paths trodden by its artists. One can see photographs, props and instruments related to this musical art form and hear various interpretations by a number of singers and writers from all generations.

"DRAGÃO DE ALFAMA" HOUSE OF FADO

"BACALHAU DE MOLHO" HOUSE OF FADO

CHANCELER YARD

"Silence, Fado is being sung". "Ah... This is Fado!" These are expressions frequently heard in Fado Houses. The atmosphere is dark and intimate emulating the music itself. Fado is heard after dinner. It's usual to have dinner served in this type of house. Here the wine becomes a good companion, able to increase the feeling of melancholy and sadness from lyrics that speak of longing, departure, sorrow, pain, loss, destiny, love, jealousy and life in general.

The performance of the genre is shared by other singers, usually two men and two women who take turns to perform songs. They are accompanied by a Portuguese Guitarist and a (regular) guitar player who know most if not all the songs. The singing of Fado is not previously rehearsed. Singers prior to singing tell musicians which piece they want and in which key. This is the simplest and most common form of hearing Fado. These houses of Fado emerged in the thirties and forties, a time when theatre, radio and cinema helped to take the genre out of alleys and neighbourhoods, bringing it to the general public. They were important for the development of the Fado genre because in order to perform in them it was necessary for one to be a a registered professional. For this reason several composers, lyricists and singers have appeared on the scene and have enriched this musical genre up to today. Now, silence... someone is about to sing Fado!

MOMENTS OF INSPIRATION

BOCAGE - POET
1765-1805

ALMADA NEGREIROS - MODERN ARTIST
1893-1970

ANA BACALHAU - SINGER
1978-...

BERNARDO SASSETTI - PIANIST AND COMPOSER
1970-2012

CARLOS PAREDES - GUITARIST AND COMPOSER
1925-2004

JOANA VASCONCELOS - CONTEMPORARY ARTIST
1971-...

MARIO CESARINY - ARTIST AND SURREALIST POET
1923-2006

RODRIGO LEÃO - MUSICIAN
1964-...

RITA BLANCO - ACTRESS
1963-...

JORGE PALMA - MUSICIAN
1950-...

JOSÉ AVILLEZ- CHEF
1979-...

RUY DE CARVALHO - ACTOR
1927-...

ANA SALAZAR - FASHION DESIGNER
1941-...

ARY DOS SANTOS - POET
1937-1984

BEATRIZ COSTA - ACTRESS
1907-1996

JOSÉ CARDOSO PIRES - WRITER
1925-1998

RICARDO ARAÚJO PEREIRA - HUMORIST
1974-...

MARIA DE MEDEIROS - ACTRESS AND DIRECTOR
1969-...

SAM THE KID - HIP-HOP MUSICIAN
1979-...

TEREZA SALGUEIRO - SINGER
1969-...

SIMONE DE OLIVEIRA - SINGER AND ACTRESS
1938-....

HERMAN JOSÉ - HUMORIST
1954-...

AGIR - MUSICIAN
1988-...

VHILS - ALEXANDRE FARTO -
CONTEMPORARY ARTIST - 1987-....

CASA FERNANDO PESSOA (FAÇADE)

RECREATION OF FERNANDO PESSOA'S BEDROOM AS BELONGING TO RICARDO REIS (CFP, GABRIELA MALDONADO E NOÉMIA ANDRÉ)

Fernando António Nogueira Pessoa (Lisbon, 1888 - 1935) better known as **Fernando Pessoa** was a Portuguese writer and poet. Within his poetry one can see Fernando Pessoa's several "personalities" into which he divided himself, all identifiable heteronyms. The **"Fernando Pessoa House"** was inaugurated in 1993 for the purpose of paying tribute to this outstanding poet. This project was brought about by the Municipality of Lisbon. They set up the centre in the Ourique "campus" neighbourhood where the writer had lived the last fifteen years of his life. It is a house with unique features reflecting the diversity in Pessoa's writing. The façade itself is decorated with his writings. The interior which gives access to the garden has an auditorium, a library devoted to poetry, show rooms, and a room that reflects the writer's world of imagery. We can find objects and furnishings belonging to the poet, and several works of art inside the house. Among other diverse activities, seminars, art exhibitions, poetry reading sessions, and guided tours are held in the house.

CASA FERNANDO PESSOA (INTERIOR)

PAGE 77→ (from up to the right)

01- PORTRAIT OF FERNANDO PESSOA, BY JÚLIO POMAR

02- PORTRAIT OF FERNANDO PESSOA, BY ALMADA NEGREIROS

03- THE GAME, SCULPTURE BY JOSÉ JOÃO BRITO

04- FERNANDO PESSOA, SCULPTURE BY LAGOA HENRIQUES

Established in 1905, The café - **"A Brasileira"** (an emblematic spot) can be found in the heart of Chiado. Due to its founder having lived in Brazil and being permitted to import items without effort, the café at first gained notoriety through the sale of genuine Brazilian coffee.

On account of its beautiful decoration and transmitted symbolism it is presently one of the busiest cafés in Lisbon. It is a meeting point for artists and among them the most famous being Fernando Pessoa. There is a bronze statue of the poet in the front patio and one can often find visitors taking pictures sitting next to him.

A BRASILEIRA (EXTERIOR) PAGE 79→ (INTERIOR)

Café **Martinho da Arcada** is the oldest café in Lisbon and dates back to 1782. It is situated in the centre of the Terreiro do Paço (Palatial Square) and was once an important place for social gatherings, gatherings that have recently resumed. Distinguished names in Portugal's cultural heritage have stopped here: Bocage, Amadeo de Sousa Cardoso, Fernando Pessoa, are among the many. The poet Fernando Pessoa and writer José Saramago (winner of a Nobel Prize for literature) are permanently reserved a table here.

Today, Café Martinho da Arcada with the Tagus River as a backdrop and its terrace under the square's arches is the ideal place to enjoy a meal or to seek sources of inspiration.

MARTINHO DA ARCADA (EXTERIOR) PAGE 79→ (INTERIOR)

MOMENTS OF INSPIRATION

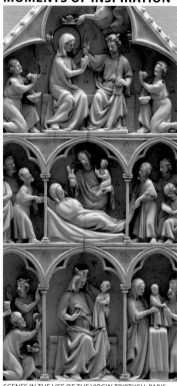

GARNITURE, DINASTIA QING

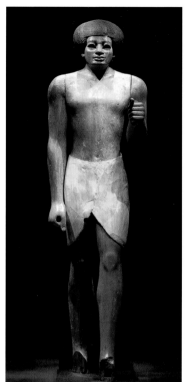

SCENES IN THE LIFE OF THE VIRGIN TRIPTYCH, PARIS

GREEK VASE, ATTICA

FUNERARY STATUE

From a will left by Calouste Sarkis Gulbenkian **Fundação Calouste Gulbenkian** (The Calouste Gulbenkian Foundation) was created. It is comprised of several areas: the museum, the foundation's headquarters, a large auditorium, areas for temporary exhibits, a library and gardens. Through the acquisition of a vast collection of magnificent works of art that he had considered as his daughters, Calouste Gulbenkian's passion for art is manifest.

Presently one can enjoy the results of his passion along a series of different halls within the museum. The first series of chambers is dedicated to Oriental and Classical Art, and is followed by galleries with Egyptian, Greco-Roman, Mesopotamian, Eastern Islamic, Armenian and Art from the Far East. The second group is of European Art (concerning Book Art), Sculpture, Painting and Decorative Arts, with emphasis given to the work of Rene Lalique. In this area one finds a wealth of artistic expression from the eleventh century up to the middle of the twentieth century.

The gardens surrounding the Foundation's buildings are truly enchanting, full of lavish vegetation and aromas. One has many options when choosing a route, be it of light, of shadows, of scents, around the Lake, or the off shoots sprouting along the side.

→ PAGES. 82/83. VIEW OVER DOWNTOWN

CALOUSTE SARKIS GULBENKIAN STATUE, BY LEOPOLDO D'ALMEIDA

FLORA, JEAN-BAPTISTE CARPEAUX

SOAP BUBBLES, ÉDOUARD MANET

PORTRAIT OF MADAME CLAUDE MONET, PIERRE-AUGUSTE RENOIR

BIOMBO "DE COROMANDEL", CHINA

Eternal Lisbon

*D*o you wish to be left at the hotel? OK. Come on, let's move on... Excuse my intruding on your conversation, but your pronunciation... indicates that you're from the North. Is this true? Oporto? Ah, I thought as much. Very good. Let's pass by Saldanha I have to greet a friend. Don't be concerned with the delay, it'll be just another luminous gesture on this dreamy morning. Forgive the literary tone that on occasion protrudes from my throat. It's almost impossible to avoid. My dream was to become a poet but I inherited from my father this green and black cab instead of blank sheets of paper. It is at this wheel that I tear paths on the road instead of ways to the heart.

Ever heard of the Farewell gentleman? He's well known here, I'd say a public figure. Almost every night he stands at that Saldanha crossing waving to passers-by. I have no idea of what binds him to making this gesture of kindness. Maybe it's his way of communicating with people. Who knows what rhythms of solitude ly behind that wave!

I have the company of my passengers, but not all are good listeners. Most just say 'good night' through gritted teeth, as if to say, I'm stuck between the walls of life, don't want to talk much less listen to you. At these times I close down my desire to share thoughts and remain thus, alone with them. If there's something that makes me uneasy is the sound of silence.

My life has not been a bed of roses but rather a sea of thorns, nevertheless even if my taxi receives 'freezing' temperatures, nothing soothes me like that warm comfort of his raised arm bidding me adieu. Each time I see him I open my window and shout out to him saying "'always, and each day". On those days I go home with lighter spirit and the walls don't cave in, they cuddle me. Then I write in green and black the most beautiful poems about kindness.

In memory of "Senhor do Adeus" Farewell gentleman - (1931-2010)

Susana Fonseca

A GINJINHA (INTERIOR)

A GINJINHA (EXTERIOR)

GINJINHA SEM RIVAL

Ginjinha is a liqueur made by fermenting fruit known as 'sour cherries'. It is usually served with some of the fermented fruit sitting on the glass's bottom, thus the reason behind the question "with or without?" meaning "with or without fruit?". Stores specialized in the drink are: "*Ginjinha Sem Rival*" - founded in the 19th century and located on *Portas de Santo Antão* street, "*Ginjinha Espinheira*" - founded in 1840 by Galician Espinheira Francisco and located in *São Domingos* Square, and "*Ginjinha Rubi*" - founded in 1931, located on *Barro Queirós* Street. Traditionally ingredients of this drink are: sour cherries, sugar, white wine, red wine, brandy and cinnamon stick. To taste *Ginjinha* at any of these popular spots is a memorable, worthwhile experience.

← PAGES 84/85. PHOTO 1 – GLORIA LIFT | PHOTOS 2/3/4 – BICA LIFT

Some were restored in hopes of recovering the popular nineteenth and twentieth century type kiosks where refreshments were sold.

Similar to their original version, the Príncipe Real Kiosk has wooden windows painted pink. The *Flores* Kiosk is all white and its roof is eggplant. The kiosk at Camões has a fully restored dome and its terrace is inviting, especially on summer nights. At these charming kiosks one can find: lemonade, cold tea mazagran, orgeat, lemon and cinnamon scented milk, currant and capilé syrups, *Ginjinha*, Port, *Moscatel* or *Beirão* liqueures. One can accompany theses beverages with chicken pies, homestyle sandwiches, and Sintra pastries *(queijadas)*, among other delicious snacks; flavours that are a flash from the past, very fresh, and without preservatives. These are refined spaces with friendly service where one can quench one's thirst. This restored Lisbon tradition with products based on natural ingredients is part of the city's charm.

LARGO DO CAMÕES

PRÍNCIPE REAL

EDUARDO VII GARDEN

AGRICULTURAL AND TROPICAL GARDEN

ESTRELA GARDEN

Gardens are scattered throughout the city and range from a more modern design to the traditional style. These are also ideal havens for days of intense heat, where one can walk and revel in nature.

Parque Eduardo VII is the largest in the city's centre. It has a huge expanse of grass, a "Cool" greenhouse with a variety of exotic plants and a heated greenhouse of warm ponds, cacti and tropical birds. Near theses greenhouses is a pond with carp and a children's playground.

The **Jardim Botânico** (Botanical Garden) - National Museum for Natural History - is a heritage of historic, cultural and scientific significance. In its vast area one can see plant species from several parts of the world.

Jardim da Estrela (Estrela Garden), later called Guerra Junqueiro Garden, has existed since the nineteenth century and is opposite to the Basilica da Estrela. Its lake with ducks and carp is a visitor attraction. The garden also has a café, flowerbeds, a gazebo, and various statues.

BOTANICAL GARDEN OF THE POLYTECHNICAL INSTITUTE

AGRICULTURAL AND TROPICAL GARDEN

BOTANICAL GARDEN OF AJUDA

"ÁGUAS LIVRES" AQUEDUCT

Águas Livres Aqueduct is a complex system for the collection, supply and distribution of water that has served the city of Lisbon from 1748 until 1967. 941 metres long and 65 metres high, the impressive stone arches that rise over the valley of *Alcântara* consist of 35 standing arches - 14 of which are ogival and the remainder being perfectly rounded.

The need for the aqueduct's construction finds its origins in a time when people settled in Lisbon and came to the conclusion that drinking water was scarce. The only area that had springs was the *Alfama* district, but these were insufficient. With the city having grown beyond its medieval walls the idea of using waters from the Carenque River Valley grew, and Romans were the first to do so.

Concern for water shortages in the city led to the implementing of food tax on meat, wine and other products in order to finance the work, but only in 1731 was the project officially started through a Royal Charter penned by King João V. Along the 19th century the aqueduct was expanded and strengthened. Nowadays one can make a guided tour of the arches along the *Alcântara* Valley.

The aqueduct is not only one of Lisbon's most notable landmarks, "ex-libris", but also one of the most remarkable works ever in hydraulic engineering. It appears in the Guinness as the largest stone arch in the world.

OUTDOOR GARDEN WITH PIECES BY RAFAEL BORDALO PINHEIRO (NSTALLATION ART: JOANA VASCONCELOS)

GALLERY

This **Museu da Cidade** (City Museum) is located at Campo Grande. It is a museum of History that aims to document and display the history of Lisbon with respect to mentality, urban, economic, political, and social development. The museum's program extends from territorial occupation during pre-history up to the onset of the Republic, in 1910.

The oldest artifacts that show the presence of occupation of the territory date back to 300,000 BC. Noteable are the plans for the construction of the Águas Livres Aqueduct, the building of the Pombaline style downtown area, and several witness accounts concerning the 1755 earthquake.

The museum's building dates back to the 17th century and is known as "Pimenta Palace". Here one should note the balance and harmony of the façade and the quality of its tile decorations. The Palace also has a forest and boxwood garden. At the edge of the woods one encounters a Pella game, which is accessed through a mall decorated with mythological figures and busts. The Boxwood Garden presently is a part of the "Bordallo Pinheiro Garden" - a set of naturalistic pieces of: fauna, flora, tiles and letters that give the garden a dreamy and 'fantastic' atmosphere.

"MERCADO DA RIBEIRA VELHA" TILE PANEL 12-13TH CENTURY

"FIGURA DE CONVITE" 18TH CENTURY

TILE PANEL (LISBONNE AUX MILLE COULEURS) DETAIL, 20TH CENTURY

The **Museu Nacional do Azulejo** (National Tile Museum) collects, preserves, studies and makes known the evolution of Ceramics and Tile. With its unique collection and activities, this museum brings to public the history of Tile in Portugal, thus bringing to the world a distinctive artistic expression of Portuguese culture.

The museum is housed in the Madre de Deus Convent in Xabregas. The convent was founded by initiative of Queen Leonor to house a group of Barefoot, Franciscan, Santa Clara nuns. The permanent exhibit spreads through various spaces of the old convent and reflects the history of tile from the 16th century to the present day.

The church, choir, St. António chapel and Queen Leonor Chapel are also part of the exhibit. On the first floor one can find rooms with tiles of "archaic" technique, archaic tiling from the 15th and 16th centuries, Enxaquetado and Mannerist Tiles from the 16th and 17th centuries, and Eastern-influenced 17th century front panels. The 2nd floor there are rooms with 18th century Dutch tile; Romantic, eclectic, and industrial tiles from the 19th and 20th centuries, and glazed tiles by modernist authors as well as modern and contemporary art from the 20th century. On the third floor is the amazing large hall with the grand view of Lisbon.

PATTERNED TILE PANEL, 16–17TH CENTURY

SANTO ANTÓNIO CHAPEL, EXTERNAL VIEW FROM NATIVITY HALL

TILE PANEL (ALLEGORY OF THE EUCHARIST) 17TH CENTURY

TILE PANEL (FLORAL VASE) 17TH CENTURY

PUNCH AND JUDY, HAND PUPPETS – ENGLAND

HORSE, STRING PUPPET – MAYANMAR

The **Museu da Marioneta** (Puppet Museum) was created in 1987 by the group "Companhia de Marionetas de S. Lourenço" and has resided at the convent - Convento das Bernardas since 2001. This is a place dedicated to the interpretation and dissemination of the history of puppetry as well as promoting this type of drama. The museum's collection includes puppets of all kinds of manipulatory technique along with masks from a variety of cultures from different parts of the world.

MUSEUM GALLERY

"VASE ADRIANO COELHO"

"VINTE ANOS DEPOIS", COLOURED LITHOGRAPH, 1903

The **Museu Bordalo Pinheiro** (Bordalo Pinheiro Museum) is a monographic museum dedicated to the work of Rafael Bordalo Pinheiro, an entrepreneur and multi-faceted artist, a remarkable figure in the public eye in Portugal of the second half of the 19th century. Bordalo Pinheiro created a vast body of work of graphic arts, visual arts, ceramics, drawings and decorative objects. Much of what he created reflects his critical view of the everyday cultural, political and social environment at the time in which he lived. At the core, and most representative of the museum's collection, is the focus on the artist's graphic work. He gained claim as a cartoonist, noteworthy is the figure of Zé Povinho, an allegory and chariacature for "The People".

"A Arte Popular" é,
sobretudo, ornamental;
é, antes de mais uma alegoria
de cores ou de tons vivos,
que enche a figuração geométrica
dos símbolos."

Luís de Pina, *Arte e Vida do Povo Português*, pág.70

"MINHO, CAIXA DE BRINQUEDOS DE PORTUGAL", BY TOMÁS DE MELO AND MANUEL

"OS CONSTRUTORES DO MAP, UM MUSEU EM CONSTRUÇÃO", POPULAR TRANSMONTANA ART

"OS CONSTRUTORES DO MAP, UM MUSEU EM CONSTRUÇÃO", THE PEOPLES THEATRE

The main purpose of the **Museu de Arte Popular** (Popular Art Museum) on Brasília Avenue is to bring the history of popular Portuguese art into context. The museum promotes the collection, storage, making inventory and disclosure of that which is relevant to popular culture in Portugal. The support and dissemination of Handicrafts from the various regions of the country contribute to enhance traditional technologies.

Noteworthy with respect to exhibits are: modernist design, "stage setting", plus the wide range of furniture and wall decorations for said exhibit halls.

"LISBOA DE MIL CORES", MURAL BY PAULO FERREIRA

Lisbon Today

*E*ven though I lack your company, today being Saturday and the weather enticing, I came out for a bike ride. Presently I stopped writing so I can feel closer to you. I'm sitting somewhere in the Garcia d'Orta Gardens waiting for something extraordinary to happen.
A few months away from your return, I've done what you've asked me. I've written you a postcard from one of our favourite spots, the Parque das Nações. I'm not going to write about me nor the longing I feel. I'll write about Lisbon, our "near to perfect city". A city that still has plenty to learn, constantly changing though it remains ours. This is the city where we met, it's our city.

Before sitting down I saw the water volcanoes that you love and went to the Portuguese Pavilion. Its architecture continues to surprise me. I also went to the Oceanarium, home to marine life and family visits and that of children that get tired of seeing so many fish. I'd liked to return with you. Who knows maybe we could live here in this small "island" which seems different from the city's centre.

When you return it is almost certain that my search for perfection will dwindle simply because you'll be here. We can follow shadowy alleys that give voice to those who have none, and if people foolishly sing, holding hands we'll join them. If our esplanade is crowded with tourists who revel in the city's warmth we'll go to the next one and perhaps discover a new angle of Lisbon which until now had remained hidden from our eyes.
Then we'll take our fill of art at the Berardo museum, the Chiado Museum , and MUDE, to later on fill ourselves with courage to paint a mural that embraces the city with the same generosity of Cristo Rei (Christ the King). When I'm with you the Tagus gives off a scent of carnations along its banks and the Belém Tower is dressed in green, your favourite colour. The Jerónimos Monastery smiles at us as we become giants in contrast to the monument that shrinks before our eyes.

If it rains we take shelter under Lisbon skies, a sky of uncertainty that needs our presence in order to make sense.

Susana Fonseca

VASCO DA GAMA BRIDGE

The **Parque das Nações** (Park of Nations) is currently the name of the place where the notorious World Expo 1998 was held. This event led to the revitalization of the area east of the city turning it into a prestigious cultural centre dominated by modern architecture with housing and business. This area of open spaces and places to walk outdoors brought a new dynamic to the city.

If we access this area through the Oriente Station, designed by Spanish architect Santiago Calatrava, we are faced with the towering iron arches, and the impressive columns and arches of reinforced concrete. Walking through innovative Shopping centre "Vasco da Gama" we see the Atlantic Pavilion and the Pavilion of Portugal. The later is by Portuguese architect Álvaro Siza Vieira.

It bares the impressive concrete visor that resembles a sheet of paper placed on two bricks.

Here we can also visit the Pavilion of Knowledge - a museum of science and technology, with interactive exhibits. One of the most visited places and attractions of this park is the Oceanarium - one of the largest aquariums in the world. It recreates for visitors four oceans, where there are sharks, barracudas, stingrays and mantarays. We can also ride the chairlift and admire the Vasco da Gama Tower, the tallest building in the city at 142 metres. The numerous gardens each with its charm, the many terraces facing the river and various buildings that comprise this space making it one of the nicest parts of town.

← *PAGES 96/97. RUA DA GLÓRIA*   → *PAGE 99. GARE DO ORIENTE STATION / VIEW OF THE TAGUS RIVER AT THE "PARK OF NATIONS" / ATLANTIC PAVILION*

LISBON TODAY

OCEANARIUM

ROSSIO DOS OLIVAIS

WATER VOLCANO

ALAMEDA DOS OCEANOS

OCEANARIUM

CHRIST THE KING

The monument to **Cristo Rei** (Christ the King) first opened in Almada in 1959. In 1934 a former Cardinal, Patriarch of Lisbon, was impressed with the imposing image of Christ the Redeemer of Corcovado during a visit to Brazil and thus came about the idea of building the said monument. The Shrine of Christ the King became a historical reference of spirituality during the first half of the twentieth century in Portugal. Being a place of prayer, presently the monument is also a beautiful viewpoint of the city of Lisbon.

The **"25 de Abril" Bridge**, officially called The Tagus Bridge and formerly known as Salazar Bridge, opened in 1966. Crossing the Tagus river estuary it is a suspension bridge that connects the cities of Lisbon and Almada. It was considered the fifth longest suspension bridge in the world at the time of its inauguration. Every year on the ides of March the bridge is closed to traffic so as to hold the Lisbon Half Marathon.

"25 DE ABRIL" BRIDGE

É INOVADOR.

TORNA O PRODUTO ÚTIL.

É ESTÉTICO.

AJUDA O PRODUTO A SER ENTENDIDO.

NÃO ATRAPALHA.

É HONESTO.

É DURÁVEL.

É CONSISTENTE ATÉ AO ÚLTIMO DETALHE.

PREOCUPA-SE COM O MEIO-AMBIENTE.

O MENOS DESIGN POSSÍVEL

MUDE, the Museum of Design and Fashion is in the centre of the Pombaline downtown area and has one of the largest collections of couture and furniture - the Francisco Capelo collection. This museum aims to be much more than a space with a collection of product design samples and fashion. The MUDE aims to equate the concept of design in its various forms within the twentieth century and show new trends in design of the 21st century. It is a place where variables such as: creative experimentation, industrial production, the relationship between design / art / crafts, environmental and technological challenges are the subject of reflection.

← *PAGE 104 GALLERY*

PIECES ON DISPLAY AT THE MUDE GALLERY

(BERARDO MUSEUM) BELÉM CULTURAL CENTRE

The **Museu Colecção Berardo** (Berardo Collection Museum), opened in 2007, is a museum for Modern and Contemporary Art. This museum is housed at the Exhibition Centre of Centro Cultural de *Belém (CCB)* and has over 800 works of art.

The museum's programming makes use of rotation and thus displays the various artistic movements found within the collection. Art from the 20th and early 21st century, through movements such as: Surrealism, Pop Art, Hyper-realism, Minimal and Conceptual art can be viewed therein. The museum's permanent exhibit, along with temporary exhibitions, allows a cultural dynamic that attracts a diverse audience and helps make Lisbon a destination for cultural tourism.

TEMPORARY EXHIBITION, JOANA VASCONCELOS

(BERARDO MUSEUM) BELÉM CULTURAL CENTRE

DIANE ET ACTÉON, 1991-92

TEMPORARY EXHIBITION, JOANA VASCONCELOS

BERARDO MUSEUM GALLERY

OPENING ENTRANCE - HALL

HALL OF OVENS

GALLERY

The **Museu do Chiado** (Chiado Museum), situated in the city's historic centre gathers, preserves and presents a collection of Portuguese art belonging to the period between 1850 and the present. Its goal is to be pivotal within the panorama of modern and contemporary art, and to foster confrontation with artistic practices of other nationalities.

The museum's collection is comprised of paintings, sculpture, sketches, video and other media. It has a program of temporary exhibitions that uses any of the following three guidelines: the core body of work, artists and movements represented in the collection, and international exhibits that intersect with the museum's collection of works by international artists.

Worth note inside the building is the "Hall of Ovens", built between 1830 and 1840 to house a set of brick ovens.

"GUAXINÃO" (BIG RACOON) BY BORDALO II, GALERIA DE ARTE PERIFÉRICA, CENTRO CULTURAL DE BELÉM

Urban Art is manifest in various public spaces in Lisbon, making known forms of artistic expression that surprise us with their implicit messages. It is through graffiti, posters, stickers, installations or other art forms that passersby find a city that wishes to be stripped of bias.

Abandoned buildings come to life with colour, beauty and poetry thanks to the talent of Portuguese and foreign artists. These works of art do not go unnoticed. Other smaller works also attract attention such as graphics on tiles or small *Barcelos* roosters that appear in uncanny places.

MURALS BY VHILS (ALEXANDRE FARTO), ALCÂNTARA (TOP) AND CHIADO (BOTTOM)

FLAMINGOS

TOURIST TRAIN

ELEPHANTS

The Zoo can be found in an area known as *Sete Rios*. It has approximately 2,000 animals from around the planet. In addition to promoting recreational and educational activities, the zoo also plays as a central role for conservation, breeding and reintroduction of endangered species into the wild.

Some of the Zoo's attractions are the Aerial lifts, Dolphin Tank, the feeding of the sea lions, the train, the reptile abode and "The Small Farm" *(quintinha)*.

→ *PAGE 111 GIRAFFES, DOLPHINS, SEALS*

Beyond Lisbon

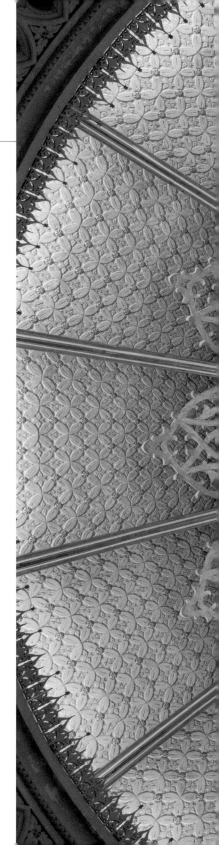

My letter to you:

*T*he changing moons bring about little change in the dark rustling of the road that leads to Sintra. Whomsoever dares to go thereupon senses that they go beyond a frontier and henceforth proceed in tacit agreement between Man and Nature. The first part obeys the laws of silence whereas the second, as an absolute monarch reigns ominously, using a voice comprised of the very sounds that shake the earth.

It was on a night with the moon dressed in white that I ventured into the Sintra hills in search of a gesture from your arms, arms that have now without explanation left me in a desert. Maybe it was an act of madness, impulse or something beyond my reckoning that simply dragged me down the road. I knew deep inside I would not find you there.

I stopped the car near a rock but the trees continued to pass me by. I stepped outside and sensed the smell of blood and resin. I saw a lady wearing lunar colours. She carried a jug under her arm and moaned like a wounded animal. I approached. She looked at me as to beg for help. Zaida was her name as she told me in a sweet voice that she knew I'd arrive.

She wished to take water to her noble lover who lay injured inside the cave, but he was unable to move. It was then that I noticed a spot of blood covering the left side on her chest.

I grabbed the jug and went into a cave lit by torches. I did the lady's asking. Her beloved drank greedily until sated. He offered me some water that was left and asked me to stay a little longer by his side. I sat next the injured man and my eyes grew heavy. I slumbered in a deep sleep, lulled by a gentle voice. I awoke with a flood of light from the sun's rays that tore through the walls of the cave and seeped into ground.

I stepped outside. My car was there. There was no evidence of the maid nor the man I had sated. I no longer sensed the smell of blood and felt strangely comforted. I found not your arm's gesture, but something impelled me to write you this letter.

Your's A.

This letter was found at Cova da Moura (Moor Cave), Sintra, on November 1, 2009.
Susana Fonseca

COLARES

Sintra's forests, the seas and cliffs form a lovely setting where you can take strolls in Europe's most sun exposed country.

Ericeira is a very old tourist town dating back to 1000 B.C. It belongs to the municipality of Mafra. According to legend it got its name due to the abundance of hedgehogs in the region. The town developed through the fishing industry and due to the importance of its port

Praia Grande is one of the best known in Sintra's district. With an extensive beach it has favourable conditions for surfing and bodyboarding. It is also well known for dinosaur footprints which are visible on the bedrock at the bottom of the beach.

GRANDE BEACH

GUINCHO BEACH

← PAGES112/113. MONSERRATE PALACE - SINTRA

CABO DA ROCA

ERICEIRA

BOCA DO INFERNO

The western most tip of continental Europe is located in Cabo da Roca, lying within Sintra's hills, at the parish of Colares.

The Cabo da Roca lighthouse is situated on a cliff approximately 140 metres high. It is a starting point for many eco-trails that allow you to enjoy spectacular scenery. The beach Praia das Maçãs (Apple Beach) is a small beach with stores next to it. It's also known as the Banzão streetcar terminal, having resumed its fuction in 1980.

The extensive coastline next to Lisbon entices one to visit its beaches, to enjoy sunbathing, swimming, and the unforgettable landscape.

Guincho Beach is held as one of the best places in the world for water sports such as windsurfing.

The "Boca do Inferno" (Hell's Mouth) is located on the west coast of Cascais and is renown for its Dantesque like scenery, especially when the sea is turbulent. Not lacking bars or restaurants to serve visitors, the beaches at Costa da Caparica are quite busy along their 15 kilometres long extention.

COSTA DA CAPARICA

MAFRA CONVENT FAÇADE

25 kilometres from Lisbon, the **Palácio Nacional de Mafra** (Mafra National Palace) is located within the township of Mafra. Also called the Mafra Royal Convent, it was built by King João V to fulfill a vow of succession. This is the most important of Portuguese Baroque monuments. It encompasses a basilica, a royal palace and a convent of the Order of St. Francis.

German goldsmith Johan Friedrich Ludwig, trained as an architect in Italy, was in charge of this work which began in 1717 and finished in 1770, mobilizing tens of thousands of workers and teachers of the various arts, a work considered as the seed for the first school of sculpture in the country.

On the king's 41st birthday, 22 October 1730, was the solemn inauguration of the basilica, festivities that lasted a week. The building houses one of the most significant Portuguese libraries. It has approximately 40,000 volumes and numerous works of art commissioned by the monarch. The library's books deal with topics such as Civil and Ecclesiastical Law, Medicine and Physics. Some say that bats residing therein aid in the conservation, preventing the destruction of works by moths.

There are many legends regarding the convent, the most popular of these relating to the existence of huge rats in the palace's underground.

The Mafra National Palace was classified as a National Monument in 1910 and was finalist upon the election of the Seven Wonders of Portugal, in 2007.

LIBRARY

SINTRA NATIONAL PALACE (EXTERIOR)

SINTRA PALACE INTERIOR

Palácio Nacional de Sintra (Sintra National Palace) is located in the historic centre of Sintra. It was built upon a former royal Muslim residence, having become the property of Portuguese kings for over eight centuries. The present building underwent successive modifications. King Manuel I ordered the construction of the east wing, well known for its exquisite window ornamentation. It was also this monarch's initiative to build the tower for the Blazon Hall of Arms, and the redecorating of the palace with coats of existing tile giving it its singular Mudejar character that it still preserves today. During his reign there were several evening feasts in the presence of the king himself with Moor musicians and artistic figures from court - Gil Vicente for instance.

The palace has been inhabited for long periods time, either to provide support for hunting, or as a refuge from Lisbon during the summer months. The interior has collections of furniture, paintings, ceramics and textiles dating from the 16th to the 19th century.

There are several halls endowed with specific features that leave visitors enchanted. The kitchens are especially known for their conical chimneys of monumental proportions. Its 'profile' has long been a distinguishing characteristic marking Sintra's landscape; a town along with its collection of monuments classified in 1995 by UNESCO as being World Heritage of Humanity.

ADAMASTOR

PENA PALACE (INTERIOR)

PENA PALACE

KITCHEN

Palácio da Pena (Pena Palace) was built by D. Fernando Coburg-Gotha in the nineteenth century. Influenced by the eclectic and Romantic trends of the time, D. Fernando II, married to D. Maria II, chose a revivalist palace with the artistic traditions from antiquity to the Renaissance. In addition we find the influence of Eastern art, domes, minarets and Mudejars, and the decorative Manueline style. To oversee the work the Baron of Eschwege was summoned, he in turn was inspired by the palaces of Bavaria. At 500 metres of altitude the Pena Palace comprises the most complete and admirable example of Portuguese Romantic architecture, warming hearts of fantasy as if it were the sun itself. From the Palace the visitor can see Pena Park, a blanket of trees that entices one to walk through idyllic paths of numerous gardens among other pleasures worthy of royalty.

TILE PANEL

MOOR CASTLE

Castelo dos Mouros (Moor Castle), also called Sintra Castle, is most likely of Muslim foundation, dating from the ninth century. It was erected on a massive rocky ridge on Mount Sintra. Being surrounded by countryside, the town of Sintra and Pena Palace; the view from the top of its walls is outstanding. Due to its purpose which is not so much to defend the village but the defense and surveillance of Lisbon, and her surroundings; no battle was ever fought in this castle. In 1154 King Afonso Henriques gave the village a Foral for municipal foundation. With the continuous advancement and Reconquest to the South, Moor Castle lost its strategic importance and eventually came to be abandoned during the Second Dynasty. It was temporarily inhabited by Jews at the end of the 14th century, who eventually left due to the expulsion of ethnic and religious minorities. Ruins due to the passage of time, coupled with damage that arose during the 1755 earthquake came to emphasize the abandonment of the castle. By the19th century King Fernando proceeded to fully restore of the old fortress meaning that currently, little can be seen of the original castle, with exception to the base of the towers and walls. Moor Castle and its storage tank has been classified as a National Monument since 1910.

MONSERRATE PALACE (EXTERIOR)

The **Palácio de Monserrate** (Monserrate Palace) is part of Monserrate Park. This palace was designed in mid-nineteenth century by English architect James T. Hair Knowles to serve as a summer residence for the Cook family. The architect had to adapt the project to existing ruins of a neo-Gothic mansion. The building that was erected is original and eclectic. The edifice's domes, red doors and Gothic inspired windows stand out. The interiors are lush, full of eastern influences, especially in the gallery - the "Music Hall" where classical and Indian themes are combined. The superb gardens where one can find over 3000 exotic species form a magnificent whole, deserving full attention upon visit as had done poet - Lord Byron, in 1809.

MONSERRATE PALACE (INTERIOR)

REGALEIRA ESTATE

REGALEIRA MANOUR (DETAIL OF INTERIOR)

The **Quinta da Regaleira** (Regaleira Estate) is located in the historic centre of Sintra, a town classified as World Heritage by UNESCO. Built in the early twentieth century the Regaleira Estate is the result of the achieving of estate owner António Augusto Carvalho Monteiro's vision. To do so he commissioned the Italian architect and designer Luigi Manini the work. Out of the imaginings of these two figures came a summation of varied artistic trends, with particular emphasis on the Gothic, Renaissance and Manueline, while not forgetting to reminisce in the nation's historic mythical and esoteric tradition.

Regaleira has within it a palace, chapel, stables and various underground buildings. It is a surprising and unforgettable monument where one can behold a world full of symbols.

PAGE 122 ← (from up to the right)

01- INITIATION WELL, QUINTA DA REGALEIRA

02- MOORISH STYLE FOUNTAIN

03- SINTRA TRAM

04- CASCADE IN SINTRA MOUNTAIN RANGE

THRONE ROOM

The **Palácio Nacional de Queluz** (Queluz National Palace) is one of the finest Portuguese palaces and has extraordinary gardens. It was built by King Pedro III in 1747 under the direction of architect Mateus Vicente de Oliveira. It was the favourite summer residence for the royal family at the end of the 17th century. The palace is often compared to Versailles although it has many Portuguese characteristics and its scale is so different.

It is surrounded by fifteen hectares of gardens which in turn are embellished by numerous lakes, plus stone and lead sculptures from Italy and England that provide visitors with a journey through Ancient Classical Mythology. The upper gardens were designed by French architect-sculptor Jean-Baptiste Robillion and show a strong French influence.

Several thematic locations are highlighted as follows: the "Jardim Novo" or Malta Garden, Pênsil or Grand Garden, the Great Cascade, Lakes of Neptune, Amphitrite of Medals, and the Tile channels.

It has served for leisure and entertainment to the royal family whom had attended there shows of fire works, bullfights, and games of chivalry known as *Cavalhadas*.

Presently in the summer these palatial gardens remain a privileged space for the conducting of outdoor events such as musical performance, and dance among others. The Portuguese School of Equestrian Art performs equestrian activities at its New Riding Arena.

QUELUZ NATIONAL PALACE

CASCAIS BAY

MARINA DE CASCAIS

The **Cascais Marina** is home to numerous luxury yachts. It also has shops, diverse spots of leisure and is an international stage for sporting events. It has inclusively received a World Cup Sailing Championship. The **Bay of Cascais** has lent its name to a title of a well known song and is considered one of the most beautiful spots within the city. Both areas are great places to stroll and relax.

PAULA REGO HOUSE OF STORIES MUSEUM

The **Casa das Histórias de Paula Rego** (Paula Rego House of Stories) is a museum that shall display part of the body of work by the artist and that of her husband, Victor Willing (artist and art critic) who had died in 1988. The Museum's design is by Souto de Moura, an architect chosen for the task by the artist herself. The building has 750 m² for exhibit areas, a shop, a café and an auditorium with 200 seats. In accordance to the artist's own wishes the museum should be a space for "fun, be unpretentious, alive, full of joy and much mischief".

The collection is on a rotating basis. Paula Rego was born in Portugal but has lived and worked in London for a long time. Beyond a doubt she is one of the most prestigious national artists.

MUSEUM GALLERY

PUBLISHED BY:
Objecto Anónimo, Lda.

AUTHOURS:
Sérgio Fonseca, Susana Fonseca, Pedro Veloso

GRAPHIC DESIGN / PHOTOGRAPHERS:
Pedro Veloso, Sérgio Fonseca

WRITTEN AND EDITED BY:
Susana Fonseca

TRANSLATION:
Maria M. F. A. Costa

HISTORICALLY VALIDATED:
Jorge Pópulo
pages (6-7, 20, 25-27, 36-37)

THANKS TO:
Câmara Municipal de Lisboa, Turismo de Lisboa, EGEAC, Museu da Cidade de Lisboa, Museu Calouste Gulbenkian, Museu da Marioneta, Museu Bordalo Pinheiro, MUDE, Museu do Fado, Museu de Arte Popular, Museu Berardo, Museu de Marinha, Museu do Oriente, Casa Fernando Pessoa, Teatro da Comuna, Teatro Politeama, Teatro D. Maria II, Teatro Nacional de São Carlos, Jardim Zoológico de Lisboa, Parques de Sintra - Monte da Lua, Casa das Histórias, Oceanário, Maxime, Casa de Fados Bacalhau de Molho, Casa de Fados Dragão de Alfama, Martinho da Arcada, A Brasileira, A Ginjinha, Casa das Velas do Loreto, Luvaria Ulisses, A Vida Portuguesa, Hospital de Bonecas, Conserveira de Lisboa, Alfaiataria Piccadilly, Chapelaria do Rossio, A Carioca, Retrosaria Bijou, Casa do AlenTagus, Confeitaria Nacional, Confeitaria dos Pastéis de Belém, Livraria Bertrand do Chiado and Jorge Pópulo.

PHOTOGRAPHY CREDITS:
José Frade, 72, ; José Pessoa,12, 16; Henrique Ruas, 13, 15; Francisco Matias, 16; Pedro Ferreira, 92; Carlos Monteiro, 93; Luisa Oliveira, 71, 73; Museu da Cidade, 7, 36, 37; Museu Bordalo Pinheiro, 94

PRINTING:
Norprint.pt

FOURTH EDITION (revised and updated):
July 2016
1ˢᵗ Edition June 2011
© Objecto Anónimo, Lda.

ALSO AVAILABLE IN THE FOLLOWING LANGUAGES:
Portuguese, French and Spanish

COLLECTION JOURNEYS AND STORIES (other publications):
Douro Valley
Porto and Northern Portugal
Portugal

Maia, Portugal
info@objectoanonimo.com
www.objectoanonimo.com

ISBN 978-989-8256-11-9
Depósito Legal 327416/11

Find more books and other products at:

FROM PORTUGAL.com

Join us on Facebook feeds and you will be the first to know all the news and activities in Portugal:
www.facebook.com/objectoanonimo

facebook.